The
Funniest
Things . . .

The Funniest Things . . .

*I ever heard,
or saw,
or smelled,
or tasted,
or touched,
or read*

Stephen Francis

Words of praise for Stephen Francis and his first two books:

"WOW! A SECOND BOOK ALREADY! I haven't finished the first one yet."
—Mackie MacGregor

"THE FUNNIEST THINGS . . . what a great idea for a second book. I'm really glad I thought of it." —Jane Burke, author's wife

"TWENTY-FOUR DAMN PICTURES in the first book and I'm not in even one. What the hell's up with that?" —Conor Flanary

"THIS GUY WROTE ANOTHER BOOK? Did anyone actually buy the first one?"
—Slim Hoechstein, western Ohio book critic

"I LAUGHED MY ASS OFF. '. . . and if Duffy should appear . . .' is truly funny. So is 'The Funniest Things . . . .' I can't wait to read it." —Rick Kruse, book editor

"I WAS A BIT DISAPPOINTED IN THE FIRST BOOK, but I'm sure the second one will be better. It's gotta be, doesn't it?" —Fran Dunning

"I'VE READ LOTS OF BOOKS IN my day. Honest. ". . . and if Duffy should appear . . ." is full of really interesting stories and characters. I understand that Stephen's second book is even funnier than the first. I hope I'm in the second book a little more."
—Will Fitzpatrick

"THE FUNNIEST THINGS . . . is truly a work of beauty. A stroke of genius. I defy anyone to actually go through these stories and jokes and not laugh out loud. It is destined to go down in literary circles as an American masterpiece."
—Jack Tripper, Entertainment Weakly website

"MARVELOUS! BLOCKBUSTER! WHAT a wonderful story about growing up. There are so many events that happened to Stephen Francis that I could relate to. Anybody who grew up in the sixties or seventies, anybody who went to Catholic school, or anyone who played high school athletics will surely find a great deal of nostalgia in this book."
—Bill Klein

"IT WASN'T EASY FINDING PEOPLE TO COMMENT ON either of these two books, so I will. They are fun, interesting, easy reads. The books are filled with great, unique, and very funny characters. I often ask myself where I would be without the Fran Dunnings, Will Fitzpatricks, Conor Flanarys, and Mackie MacGregors of the world? I'd probably be a real professional writer by now, but it's sure been a fun ride with those guys. Hey, read the books! Understand, of course, that the second book is definitely "R" Rated, so if you were looking for all clean stuff, go put this book away and find a copy of '. . . and if Duffy should appear . . .'"   —Stephen Francis, author

"I REALLY ENJOYED YOUR BOOK. It was very interesting. I think you're the smartest person I know."   —Ric Stenson, Lyndonville, Vt.

"THE FIRST BOOK IS VERY WELL DONE. It's cute, interesting, poignant, heart-warming. The second book is flat-out funny as hell. The stories and the jokes . . . . I laughed until I cried. I will say this . . . it IS sort of a guys' book."
—Sue Schnipke, book critic

Library of Congress Control Number: 2007907306
ISBN: Hardcover   978-1-4257-8422-5
                   Softcover   978-1-4257-8410-2

This book was printed in the United States of America.

To order additional copies of this book, contact:
Xlibris Corporation
1-888-795-4274
www.Xlibris.com
Orders@Xlibris.com
37932

Contents

SECTION III

. . . . *Then College Was Freaking Hilarious*

SECTION IV

Funny Doesn't Stop When You Grow Up

SECTION V
The Funniest Thing . . . .

Acknowledgements

There are a number of people I need to thank. First, I need to thank my wonderful wife Jane for all of her help in the composing and printing of this manuscript and all of my other writings. Your help is invaluable and much needed. My editors, Frank Coughlin and Rick Kruse, once again did a fine job, and I appreciate their efforts. I need to thank all of my friends who continue to be sources of humor. I've laughed an awful lot WITH you and AT you, and you make life bearable. My family, of course, has been and continues to be a great source for humor. I'd like to particularly thank a very fine friend, Duane Ressler, who contributed one of the greatest chapters in this book.

Finally, I'd like to thank the good people at Xlibris Press for their cooperation in the publication of this book.

Read and enjoy.

Introduction . . . .

And Warning from the author

Let's get something straight right now. This book is rated "R" (racy, raunchy, and really, really funny). It is not intended for young people or for people with sensitive feelings about humor. Many of the stories are very mild in nature, but there are plenty of stories that include language not fit for genteel society. Turn the pages at your own risk. If you are offended by bad language and coarse (but very funny!) subject matter, then this book is probably not for you. Put it down. Go away. I strongly suggest you purchase and read my first book, ". . . and if Duffy should appear . . ." which is also very funny, but doesn't include hardly any bad language.

Here's what you are going to get in this book: I am going to relate to you the funniest things that ever happened to me or that I ever heard, smelled, touched, tasted, read, etc. I will follow the personal chapters with some of my favorite jokes. Whenever possible I will tell you the origin of the joke; when and where I heard it, who I was with, and any other pertinent details. This way, I hope you will be able to meet and enjoy some of the very funny people I've known throughout my life.

Some of the jokes were sent to me through e-mail, but most of them have been collected through the years. I won't really attempt to categorize the humor because, to me, some things are just damn funny and they don't really fit into a category. Go ahead and laugh out loud and go ahead and steal any of these jokes and retell them. If you are married, read the jokes aloud to your wife (make sure she is listening) and then let me know if she thinks they're funny. My guess is that more men will think these are funny than women, but I guess we'll see.

Section I

The Family That Laughs Together . . . .

1

"Yeah But That's A Lot Of Money"

I've always wanted to write a book about humor. You know, all the funny stories and jokes I've ever heard. I know hundreds of people who have told me over the years, "I really love jokes. I just can't remember them."

Well, I guess I've been blessed, because I CAN remember jokes. I have a mental filing system in my head that allows me to remember not only jokes, but also the funniest things that ever happened to me, my friends, and my family. I'm not sure that my family, as a whole, would be considered particularly funny by most people, but I disagree. My two brothers and two sisters are incredibly funny—if not in telling jokes, then certainly in the things they've done that I have been a part of or witnessed. Want an example? OK.

My father, a great man who taught me many things, died in 1991. That's not very funny, is it? Well, the next Christmas my mother sent all five of us (my brothers and sisters) cards with a five hundred dollar check from my father's estate. All five siblings have two children, and it was my mother's wish that we do something nice for our families. Two days after receiving my card with the check I called my brother Jack who lives in Glendale, Arizona. We are pretty close and speak frequently.

Anyway, in the midst of our conversation I asked him if he had received the card from our mother. He said that he had. I asked him what he thought about the money. He said, "Hey, it's mom's money and I guess she can do anything she wants with it."

"Yeah, but I think $1000 is a lot of money for her to be sending to each of us," I said. There was dead silence on the other end of the line. Total silence for about five seconds. "How much did you get?" Jack asked me.

"I got $1000. Why, how much did you get?"

He said, "I got $500."

"Get out. Why would she send me $1000 and you only $500? Everybody knows that you were always mom's favorite." (The other four of us still insist that's true) I took a real shot in the dark and said, "Besides, I talked to Julia (my younger sister) this morning and she got $1000, too." At this point I was trying my hardest to not laugh or give away my practical joke. The conversation went on for about ten more minutes, and I spent time planning to call Julia immediately and get her in on the joke. Heck, I thought I might be able to get every other sibling involved. Either that or I would pull the same joke on them. That was even better, I decided.

Unfortunately, my goody-two-shoes wife was listening and she nearly ripped the phone out of my hand insisting that I tell the truth. I eventually did. I think that was really funny while it lasted. Wasn't it?

That night as I tried to get to sleep I laughed to myself and was reminded about two things. First, if something is truly funny, you can recall it later that day or even the next day or week or month or year and immediately laugh out loud even if you only remember the punch line. Second, words that my father spoke to me about forty years ago. He said, "You know, Stevie, nobody likes a smart ass." Really? I guess we'll find out in the rest of this book.

Concerns At The Physical

An elderly married couple scheduled their annual medical exams on the same day so they could travel together. The man was examined first, and when the doctor finished the exam he asked the old guy if he had any concerns or questions.

"As a matter of fact, I do," said the old guy. "After I have sex with my wife, the first time I'm always hot and sweaty and after the second time I'm always cold and chilly. What's up with that?"

The doctor had no answer. After examining the old woman the doctor said, "Everything seems to be fine. Do you have any questions or concerns?"

The lady just shook her head. The doctor then said, "You know your husband had a serious and unusual concern. He claims that he is hot and sweaty after having sex with you the first time, and cold and chilly after having sex with you the second time. Do you have any idea why?"

"Oh, that crazy old fart. That's because the first time is on the 4th of July and the second time right around Christmas."

Barroom Bets

I had forgotten this joke until I was reminded of it on a flight to Florida with an old friend during the summer of 2007. I was telling him about the concept for this book and he started laughing. I asked him why he was laughing and he reminded me of the two funniest jokes he had ever heard, and I had told him both. Here's the first.

A sharp-looking guy with a tweed sport coat and a handle-bar mustache was sitting in a bar having a beer when the guy sitting next to him asked him what he did for a living.

"I win bar bets," replied the first guy.

"Bar bets? How do you make a living doing that?" asked the second guy.

"Let me show you," said the first guy. "I'll bet you, oh, let's say $50, that I can bite my eye."

"Bite your eye? How the hell . . . you're on," says the second guy.

The first guy reaches up, pops a fake eyeball out of its socket, puts it near his mouth, and bites down carefully. The second guy is astonished, but he pays the bet. A few minutes later he looks over at the shark and asks, "What else ya got?"

"Well," says the shark deep in thought. "I'll bet you another $50 that I can bite my other eye."

The second guy stares at him for a few minutes. He thinks to himself, 'There's no way he could have two fake eyes. How could he possibly bite his other eye?' He agrees to the bet, at which point the shark reaches up, takes out his dentures, and carefully bites his other eye. He collects the bet, but now the second guy is really steamed. He wants to get back at the shark. "What else ya got?"

The shark thinks for a few minutes then says, "I'll bet you $500 that I can stand on this bar, and pee all over the bar while the bartender cheers and applauds."

Now the second guy can't wait to see this happen. He just knows that the bartender will kill the guy if he even attempts this. "You're on," he says as they shake hands.

The shark steps up on the bar and places an empty shot glass about ten feet away. He whips out his penis and starts to spray away, aiming in the general vicinity of the empty shot glass, but his stream falls well short, getting the entire bar soaked. The bartender is standing behind the bar clapping and cheering, and when the guy finishes the bartender starts to clean up while accepting congratulations from the other patrons. The second guy can't believe what he just saw. "What the hell just happened here?"

The shark jumps down off the bar, collects his $500 and says to the loser, "A little while ago I bet the bartender $100 that I could piss into a shot glass from ten feet away."

2

Is It Possible To Be This Dumb?

In this next section it is very important to understand that times have changed a great deal from the 1960's to now. Just about everything has changed, which is sometimes good and sometimes not-so-good.

One day in 1964 or so, a student at St. Mary's Academy brought a gun to school. Obviously, in our society today this is certainly no laughing matter, but back then things were done a little differently. Someone told one of the nuns at the school that Gino had a gun. She confronted him, and, sure enough, he had a snub-nosed 32 caliber pistol with him in the school. He wasn't going to use the gun; he just brought it to school to show off. Things like that seemed to happen more in the '60's.

My brother Jack saw the nun take the gun from Gino and put it in her desk. Later in the day Jack went to the nun's desk and took the gun for himself. He had no reason to want a gun, but, well, he was Jack Francis and he did things like that. Besides that, he thought, why does the nun need a gun? He took the gun home and showed it to my oldest brother, Bob. Bob asked Jack if the gun worked, and Jack said that he had no idea, so Bob, ever the tinkerer and experimentor, decided to find out if the gun worked.

After purchasing some bullets, the two of them went out to the wooded area a couple of blocks from our house. They taped the gun to a tree, tied a string to the trigger, and backed away from the tree. Bob pulled the string. He figured he had it set just right. Nothing happened. Jack went to the tree to see what was wrong, and, just as his head was a foot or so away from the gun, Bob tried the string again, and, sure enough, the gun fired.

Jack was, needless to say, upset. Of course he couldn't hear Bob's explanation of why he had done that—his ears were ringing for a few days from being so close to the shot!

The gun stayed in our house for months and even years, and Jack tells me that he still has the gun.

One day when she was seven or eight years old my sister Julia went down to the basement of our house to Bob's "workshop." He had an area in the basement that was just called 'The Shop,' where he stored tools and all sorts of other things. In fact, if there was ever anything that you needed, you could probably find it in 'The Shop.' Julia found more than she bargained for.

Bob was working nights for the City of Lorain at the time, and he was in to all sorts of interesting activities. He also possessed a gun (a family dispute arises when this incident is brought up. The dispute is whether or not the gun Julia found was Jack's original .32 caliber or another gun that Bob owned). Anyway, Julia found the gun, which, of course, happened to be loaded with the safety off.

I ask you . . . . Is it possible to be this dumb?

Julia picked the gun up, looked at it for awhile and eventually pulled the trigger. The bullet passed through wood near Bob's shop, ricocheted off the cement basement floor, and stuck in the first-floor beams.

Everyone was scared and my parents were not very pleased that Bob had a loaded gun in the house. Well, would you be?

Here are some national "Is It Possible To Be This Dumb?" incidents.

1. A medical student doing a rotation in toxicology at a poison control center received a frantic call one day from a mother who had caught her little daughter eating ants. The intern explained to the mother that she didn't have anything to worry about, and that the ants weren't poisonous. He explained that there would be no need to bring the daughter to the hospital. The mother calmed down enough to tell the intern that she was pretty sure that the ants were dead in the girl's stomach because the mother had given the girl some ant poison to eat to be sure. At that point the intern told the mother to bring the girl to the hospital immediately.

2. A Wal-Mart employee in the Sporting Goods Department pulled a real Smooth Move. Wal-Mart employees sometimes make storewide pages, such as "I have a customer in hardware who needs help near the paints." On this particular day the page wasn't exactly as he wanted. The voice came over the storewide intercom with this message: "I have a customer by the balls in toys who needs assistance."

3. A man, wanting to rob a downtown San Francisco Bank of America, walked into the branch and wrote on a deposit slip, "This iz a stikkup. Put all the muny in

this bag." While standing in line waiting to give the teller the note, he began to worry that someone might get suspicious and call the police before he got to the front of the line. He left the Bank of America and went across the street to the Wells Fargo bank. He walked up to an empty line and handed the note to the teller. She quickly realized that he wasn't very smart and told him she couldn't accept the stickup note because it was written on a Bank of America deposit slip. He would either have to do another note on a Wells Fargo slip or he would have to return to Bank of America. The man was upset, but said, "OK," and went back across the street. The Wells Fargo teller then called the police who arrested the man while he waited in line at the Bank of America.

4. A motorist was caught by one of those automated speed traps that take a picture of the car and license and records how fast you are going. He received a picture of license and car along with a $75 ticket in the mail. Trying to be clever, he took a picture of $75 and sent it back with the ticket. A few days later he received the ticket back with a picture of handcuffs. He paid the ticket.

5. A woman called and reported that her car had been stolen. She had left her phone plugged in to the battery charger. The policeman who took the report knew exactly what to do. He called her phone in the car. The robber answered the phone and the policeman told him that he had seen the ad in the newspaper wanting to sell the car. He was interested in buying it. They arranged to meet. He arrested the thief.

3

No, Really, Nobody Likes A Smart-Ass

When he was younger my brother Jack was pretty much a wise-guy, smart-ass. That's just the way he was. It's also interesting to note that all the trouble Jack got in to as a youngster served him well when he became an Assistant Principal for a public high school. There weren't many things a kid could do that Jack hadn't already done.

Jack was expelled from St. Mary's Academy on the last day of school his junior year. My parents grounded him for the entire summer. He never went anywhere the entire summer without my parents. Every day they left a list of chores for him to complete during the day, and they expected everything to be completed by the time they arrived home from work. I will say this about Jack: he is a tireless worker, and he did the chores every day.

Jack and I also invented a game that we played for hours and hours in front of our house. Our family home was at 2021 West Erie Avenue in Lorain, Ohio. Across the street and about 150 yards away, is Lake Erie. West Erie Avenue is also Route 6, and it is a very busy street at all hours of the day. The game Jack and I invented was simple and stupid, but when you're grounded for the summer you have to come up with something interesting to do.

We would sit on the sidewalk about halfway from the front porch to the road. We were about ten yards from West Erie Avenue. We would yell at cars as they drove by to see if we could get them to respond. We had a scoring system that went something like this: one point if the person in the passing car waved, two points if he/she honked, three points if he/she honked and waved, and five points if he/she honked, waved, and yelled back at us.

Every time we played I would get the cars driven by little old ladies with their windows rolled up. I could yell as loud as I wanted, and they weren't going to respond.

No way. The next car that passed the house (we had to take turns yelling) would be filled with high school kids who would honk, yell, scream, wave, etc. It worked that way all summer, which was why Jack was the eventual champion of the game.

Another thing Jack taught me to do, either that summer or the summer before, was the apple-launch. A neighbor a few doors away had an apple tree in their backyard. We would get two-or-three foot sticks, sharpen on one end, then stab an apple with the sharp end. If we got far enough away from the houses (these were all two or three story houses, so they were quite high) we could launch, like a throw, the apples over the houses and onto passing traffic on West Erie Avenue. We would fire those things up and over the houses (it is an absolute miracle that we never broke a window in a house!) and listen for them to hit the cars or trucks. When the light at the corner was green we had to try and hit a moving target, so we had to launch the apples out in front of the cars and hope the cars would drive in to them.

Back to my brother Jack being a smart-ass. My father was a great man, but he was tough on all of us. Well, ok, he wasn't nearly as tough on me as he was on the others, but that was basically because I was never really in too much trouble, unlike my brothers. Jack was in trouble all the way through high school, and Bob was in trouble after high school.

One day Jack was sitting in the living room wearing a Wartburg College practice football jersey. My father came in, and knowing Jack's penchant for wearing clothes that, shall we say, somehow found their way to our house, said to Jack, "Hey, where'd you get that shirt?"

Jack looked at my father, looked down at the shirt, and pointed to the words on the shirt. He said, as he moved his hand in front of the letters on the shirt, "Wartburg College, Waverly, Iowa."

My father just looked at him and said, "Don't be a smart-ass."

My father sold very fine furniture for over thirty years. One day he came home from work and my brother had his feet up on the marble coffee table in front of the couch. My father looked at my brother and yelled, "Get your feet off that table." My brother just looked at him and slowly removed his feet. "How much do you think that table cost?" my father asked.

"I don't know," my brother said.

"No, really, take a guess. How much do you think that table cost? C'mon. How much?"

My brother shrugged his shoulders and said, "I don't know. A thousand dollars?"

Once again, my father looked at him and snarled, "Don't be a smart-ass."

One day my brother was in a high school religion class taught by Monsignor James J. Duffy, the crusty old Pastor at St. Mary's Parish. The old Monsignor was on his last legs and wasn't much of a teacher. He frequently called the name of a student and then told the student to read aloud. He would just look on the class roll, call a name, and go from there. He called, "Jack Francis."

My brother wasn't in a mood to read that day so he said, "He's not here today."

The crusty old Monsignor was no dummy. He responded, "All right, then you read."

My oldest brother Bob was also in plenty of trouble, but most of his trouble wasn't really very funny. Suffice to say he led a tough life and experienced many, many things.

One Sunday when I was a junior in high school we went to 9:00 church. My father told us in the car on the way home that we would grab something really light to eat and then we would go right to the tennis courts. I made the suggestion that we go ahead and eat the wonderful full brunch my mother was sure to make and THEN go to tennis courts. I pointed out that I was never very hungry after tennis, and I was really hungry right then. We got in to a bit of an argument and my father just started yelling at me. He finally said, "Sometimes you're as stupid as one and as rotten as the other," referring, of course, to my brothers.

See, Bob was the stupid one and Jack was the rotten one.

The Name Eludes Him

An elderly man had three of his friends over to play cards one night. He started telling them about a great restaurant he had taken his wife to just days before.

"What's the name of this place?" one of the others asked.

"Ahhh hell, you know me. I have a bad case of CRS. You know, Can't Remember Shit. Give me a minute, I'll think of it. What's the name of that one flower that smells really good?"

"Petunia," one guy suggests.

"Nah, hell, not Petunia. That doesn't smell good. The flower that smells good.

"Carnation?"

"Well that smells good, but that ain't it. Give me the name of another flower that smells good."

"Rose?" the third guy asks.

"Yeah, that's it. Rose. Hey, Rose," the host yells to his wife in the kitchen. "What the hell was the name of that restaurant we ate at the other night?"

4

Faroh's Finest Chocolates

There was a famous chocolate store in Lorain, Ohio when we were growing up. Faroh's Finest Chocolates was the name of the store, and it was really a treat when our family was able to afford a box of Faroh's. The Faroh's milk chocolate was particularly good, and it would just about melt in your mouth. Actually, I guess that's exactly what it did: melt in your mouth, as candy should do.

Anyway, one day my brother Jack and I noticed that my father had brought home a box of Faroh's. It was a variety box of chocolates, which meant dark chocolate, milk chocolate, and even white chocolate pieces were included in the box. We knew that for dessert that night we would get a chance to have some of this delicious candy. Jack hatched a plan and wanted to make sure I was part of it, as he often did. Misery loves company?

We went out into the yard and made some mud. The color of the mud was just about the color of the Faroh's milk chocolate. Jack formed a piece of the mud into the size of a piece of Faroh's candy. We took the fake candy into the house. The box of candy was sitting on the buffet table in the dining room. I went into the living room and started talking to my father, who was reading the newspaper and enjoying a martini. Jack opened the box of candy, removed one piece (leaving the little paper wrapper in place) and replaced the missing piece of candy with the mud square.

Dinner at our house when we were growing up was a rather formal affair. We used the big dining room every night, had cloth napkins on the table, said grace together, and then passed the food in one direction. At the conclusion of the meal we cleared the dishes and then had dessert. My father, a strict, no-nonsense-when-it-came-to-dinner guy, had told my mother that she didn't need to make any dessert, because we would be having the Faroh's Finest Chocolates.

The box was brought from the buffet table and my father got to select his piece of candy first. I sat to my father's right and Jack sat to his left, across the table from me. We held our breath as my father looked at the box of candy, hoping and praying that he wouldn't select the piece of mud. He didn't. Jack selected next. Just after he took his piece of candy from the box he said, "Wait, I got the wrong piece. That's the one I wanted." He pointed at the piece of mud. That was pure genius, as Jack knew that as soon as he said he wanted one particular piece, older brother Bob would take that very piece.

Sure enough, Bob looked at the box and said, "Yeah that does look like a good piece." He picked up the piece of mud. Jack and I looked across the table at each other. There was a moment of silence. We waited a second. Bob finally picked up the piece of mud and took a nice, healthy bite. He chewed it for a moment or two before spitting it out.

"What the . . . ." he said as he spit out the mud. Jack and I were trying to control ourselves, but to no avail. We just about lost it, laughing and pointing at Bob and the piece of mud. Our father did not really think it was funny (at least he never admitted that he thought it was funny. C'mon, how can that NOT be considered funny?)

"You know what!"

I heard this story from my oldest brother Bob at the Riviera in Las Vegas in June, 2007. It's an immediate classic.

A guy and his wife walk into a bed and breakfast in New England for a one-week stay. They check in and head through the dining room to the stairs. They notice a large parrot in a cage near the side of the room.

"Brawwkk," squawked the bird. "Hey you."

The guy looked around. "Me?" he asked.

"Brawwkk. Yeah, you."

"What?" the guy says.

"Brawwkk. Your wife is the ugliest woman in the world."

The wife was aghast, the guy upset. He went back to the front desk and told the owner what the bird had said. The owner enters the dining room and goes over and rattles the bird's cage and starts yelling at him. "I've told you before to be nice to our guests. I don't want you to ever say anything like that again. Do you hear me?" yelled the owner. He apologized profusely to the customer.

The next day the guy is walking through the dining room and again the bird says, "Brawwkk. Hey you."

The guy looks at the bird and says, "What?"

"Brawwkk. Your wife is the ugliest woman in the world."

Now the guy is really upset. He again goes to the owner and complains. The owner tries to apologize and takes the cage from its place. He takes the bird outside and tells it that if it ever says anything like that again he will kill it.

The next day the guy is walking through the dining room and the bird says, "Brawwkk. Hey you."

The guy is really anxious to hear what the bird will say this time. "What?" the guy says.

The bird pauses for a second and says, "Brawwkk . . . . You know what."

5

Absolutely The World's Worst Singer

My brother Bob is absolutely the world's worst singer. He is so bad that even if you are a good singer and singing next to him, your voice will be ruined. He's that bad.

When Bob was in 7th grade at St. Vincent de Paul School in Lorain, Ohio his teacher was Sister Mary Leo. Sister Leo was also the school's choir director, and she made every student audition for the choir. When it got to be my brother's turn to audition he said, "Sister, I really don't want to be in the choir. Besides, you've heard me sing and I can't sing."

Sister Leo was having none of that. "Everyone tries out for the choir and you are no exception. Now go to the front of the room and audition."

The audition went like this: you had to sing the song, "My Country Tis Of Thee," until Sister Leo was satisfied that you were either good enough to be in the choir or bad enough to be told to, "Sit down." Most students got to sing the entire first verse before she made a decision one way or another. Not my brother Bob.

He stood up in front of the other 28 seventh graders and began to apologize. "I, uh, really can't sing and don't really want to be up here . . ." Sister Leo sat in the back of the room and said, "Sing."

"But I'm really not a good singer. I'll never be in the choir," my brother mildly protested."

"Everyone tries out for the choir. I told you to sing. Now sing," said the mean-spirited nun.

My brother started in on the song, "My country tis of thee . . . ." He was interrupted by Sister Leo's shout of, "Sit down!" He barely got five words out before she told him to stop. The rest of the class laughed, of course, and my brother was completely embarrassed. He swears to this day that Sister Leo was just trying to embarrass him that day.

It wasn't the only day he was embarrassed as a singer.

When Bob graduated from St. Mary's High School in Lorain in 1966, he received a congressional appointment to the United States Merchant Marine Academy. When he arrived in New York he was informed that every cadet had to be involved in a number of activities. Our academies believed then, as they do now, that students should stay active and become well-rounded. Bob decided to try out for the Glee Club. The Glee Club, of course, is a musical singing group. There were really no auditions, and he joined the club.

One day the 25-or so member group was rehearsing a song the last line of which was, ". . . and Christ has died." The director was an old Austrian fellow who loved his music. As they were singing the song, something just didn't sound right on that last line. He had the group sing it over and over. He couldn't quite figure out what the problem was. Finally he said, with his heavy Austrian accent, "Ve vill sing it solo. Everyvone vill sing ze line until ve figure out ze problem."

Bob was near the middle of the group, so every singer went through the line until it was his turn. He sang, ". . . and Christ has died."

The Austrian director said, "Yah, he died. You just killed him vit that last note."

Again, total embarrassment for my brother.

The final terrible singing incident occurred in Seattle when all five of my siblings and I surprised my mother (she was visiting my sister Veronica who was living in Seattle at the time). We all arrived at different times, but we eventually gathered at Veronica's for a nice dinner and some family time. My sisters, Julia and Veronica, had re-written the song "Hello Dolly" using my mother's name. "Hello Tillie" was a really cute, funny tribute to my mother. We actually practiced singing it a few times, and during practice I could tell that Bob's singing voice hadn't improved much. However, during the actual performance it was unbelievable. We all had had a few drinks, and Bob's voice, like most men, got louder after a few drinks. Not better, just louder.

We had two rows of singers, with Julia and Veronica in the front and Bob and Jack and me in the back. The music started and we began to sing. When Bob opened his mouth I couldn't believe it. It was horrible. It was so bad that I couldn't even sing. Neither could my other brother. I actually fell over backwards I was laughing so hard. Even when I righted myself and tried to sing normally his voice was so bad that it took me off key. Our family is not known for having great singers, but this was remarkable. I have never heard anything that terrible before or since. Some of the early "American Idol" singers are pretty bad, but nobody can be as bad as my brother Bob.

The Buffalo Theory

One of the greatest programs in television history was Cheers. Mailman Cliff Clavin was a wonderful character who often espoused in-depth philosophical ideas. One of his greatest theories was called The Buffalo Theory, and he explained it to Norm while sitting at the bar.

"Ya see, Norm, it's like this. A herd of buffalo can only move as fast as the slowest buffalo. When the herd is hunted, it is the slowest and weakest ones in the back of the herd that are killed first. This natural selection is good for the herd as a whole, because the general speed and health of the entire herd is improved by the regular killing of the weakest members.

"In much the same way, the human brain can only operate as fast as the slowest brain cells. Excessive intake of alcohol, as we know, kills brain cells. Naturally, alcohol attacks the slowest and weakest brain cells first. In this way, regular consumption of beer eliminates the weaker brain cells, making the brain a faster and more efficient machine.

"That's why you always feel smarter after a couple of beers."

6

Gross Even For Me

One of the best things my parents did for me was teach me a certain amount of discipline. When I was in school (grade school and high school) I was expected to spend at least an hour every evening, Monday through Thursday, in my bedroom studying. Actually, I think they probably knew I wasn't studying all the time, but at least I was up in my room reading or whatever.

Further, one of the best things they ever did was supply me with a typewriter, which allowed me to write just about every evening. I wrote a book during my sophomore year in high school, and another during my senior year. Much of the book written during my senior year, *One Play Away*, is included in my first published book, ". . . and if Duffy should appear . . ."

So, every night after dinner I would retreat to my room and either read or write. I certainly wasn't doing homework all that time. Sometimes I would just sit up in the room and see how loud of a fart I could conjure up. Most guys will tell you that they really revel in their own farts. We despise having to smell others, but we are often very proud of our own, as long as they aren't "electric farts." You know, the kind with a little juice. By the way, when you reach fifty years old they tell you the rules of life change. For example, never trust a fart, particularly if you haven't been farting all day. In fact, if you haven't been farting all day and you have people around it is very important that you let out a "test fart." You know, to see how loud they are going to be, whether you need to 'fart and run,' whether there will be some juice with it, etc. Another rule for over fifty people: Never pass a restroom without using it. Things like that.

Anyway, one very cold evening in March of 1969 I was in my bedroom reading and farting. Two nights in a row my mother had made some absolutely delicious, fart-producing meals. The night before we had had pork and lima beans, and that night we had had stuffed cabbage. Yum, yum followed by some great explosions.

THE FUNNIEST THINGS . . .

I was trying to see how loud I could get the farts to be when the second worst thing happened. I say the second worst thing, because the worst thing that can happen when you are having a farting session is you shit your pants, but that didn't happen this time. This time, I held a fart in for a minute or two to try to build some extra explosion. The fart, when it finally came out, sounded like a sixth grade band member learning to play a long note on a trumpet. The fart lasted a full six or seven seconds. What happened next was what was gross.

The smell that came from my ass was just about the worst thing I had ever smelled. It grossed me out, and I was the farter! It must have been the combination of the lima beans and the cabbage, but whatever it was, it filled the room with a kind of green haze. My eyes started to water. My nose burned. I had one or two of those dry heave things (you know what I mean). I almost threw up right there.

My bedroom had a door going out on to a second floor porch, and I immediately opened that door. I even tried to open the painted-closed window in the room. I couldn't get rid of the smell. It was awful. I've smelled dead skunk, and this was worse. In fact, that might have been the worst-smelling thing I've ever had to breathe. Of course the next day at school I was bragging about the fart, but I will certainly never forget that smell. Some of my friends even got close to me and smelled me, thinking that the awful smell might have lingered on my clothes.

Bubba and Jimmy Joe

One day Jimmy Joe was walking down Main Street and he saw his buddy Bubba driving a brand new pick-up truck. Bubba pulled up to Jimmy Joe with a wide grin on his face.

"Bubba, where'd you get that truck?"

Bubba smiled and said, "Why Sally Mae Johnson give it to me."

"She give it to ya? I knew she was kinda sweet on ya, but she gave you a new truck? How'd that happen?"

"Well, Jimmy Joe, lemme tell you what happened. She saw me over at Snakeyes and asked me if I wanted to take a ride in her new truck. Well we wuz drivin' out on County Road Number 6 in the middle of nowhere. Ya know, out near Harper's Woods. She put on the 4-wheel drive and headed into the woods. We got pretty deep in the woods and she parked the truck, got out, threw all her clothes off and said, 'Bubba, take whatever you want.' So I took the truck."

"Bubba, you are one smart man. Them clothes never woulda fit you."

EW Internet 02-07-04

"Logic? What's that?"

Bubba and Jimmy Joe were sitting in the Snakeyes Bar one afternoon and Bubba told Jimmy Joe, "I'm gonna go to college." Jimmy Joe was shocked.

"Why you wanna go do something like that fer? Hell, you hated high school. How you think yer gonna get along in college?"

"It's gonna make me a better, more rounded person. I'm gonna go over tomorrow to the junior college and meet with some guy named Dean. He's gonna git me signed up fer some classes for the fall."

Bubba goes the next day and meets with the Dean. After meeting for awhile the Dean leaves Bubba in a room. When he returns a little while later he says to Bubba, "Well Mr. Jones, I have you all registered for classes. You will be taking a math class, a science class, a history class, and logic."

Bubba looks at him for a second and says. "I think I understand most all of those, except Logic. What's Logic?"

The Dean says, "Perhaps I can explain to you what logic is. Do you own a weed whip?"

Bubba says, "Yeah, I got me a weed whip."

The Dean says, "Then you must own a yard."

"Yeah, I got me about a acre of yard."

The Dean continues. "If you have a yard, then you must own a house."

"Yeah," Bubba nods. "I got me the old Jameson place out on County Road Z."

"And if you own a home, then you must be married."

"Yep," Bubba says. "Been married to my cousin Donna fer nine years."

"And if you're married," says the Dean, "then I can logically deduce that you are a heterosexual."

Bubba looks at him dumbfounded and says, "Damn. That's logic, huh?"

That night Bubba meets Jimmy Joe at Snakeyes. Jimmy Joe wants to know how things went for Bubba at the college.

Bubba tells Jimmy Joe, "Everythin went fine. I got registered fer four classes. Math, Science, History, and Logic."

Jimmy Joe looks at Bubba and says, "Logic? What's that?"

Bubba is very proud of himself and says to Jimmy Joe, "Perhaps I can explain it to you. Do you own a weed whip?"

Jimmy Joe shakes his head and says, "Nope. Don't got me one of them."

Bubba says, "Then yer a queer."

7

Slip Of The Tongue

My wife, Jane Burke, is one of the nicest, most wholesome people I know. For her to be included in this book is truly unusual, but she relayed to me the most embarrassing moment in her teaching career, and it was a beauty.

Jane was an eighth grade teacher at St. Augustine School in Napoleon, Ohio for years. She actually left St. Augustine and then returned a few years later as the Principal, but this story deals with when she was a teacher. There were two young men in her eighth grade class one year with terrible tempers. They also didn't get along very well. I should point out that one of the boys was the son of the Principal of the school at the time, and the other young man was the son of a professional psychologist. Wouldn't you think that these kids would behave? Well, their tempers frequently got the best of them.

One morning, just before the class was to go to lunch, they started an argument with each other. No punches were thrown, but loud, obscene words were exchanged. Before my wife could separate the two, one called the other one a "mother fucker." The other responded with, "Oh yeah? You're a mother fucker, too."

My wife jumped in and yelled, "All right, that's it! We are going to stop this immediately. We're not going to put up with language like that. Settle down. You will both be going to the office. Right now it's time for lunch. Everyone bow your heads and let's say grace." (At Catholic schools they still pray a lot—morning, lunch, late in the day, etc.)

My wife started off with the sign of the cross, but instead of saying, "In the name of the Father, and of the Son, etc." she said, "In the name of the Mother . . . ." No way could she regain control of that class at that time. Eighth graders just love to lose control, and the kids in that classroom lost control, and boy was my wife embarrassed.

Beer, Cigar, Lottery Ticket

I heard this joke years ago and it has been passed around and is resurrected about every five years.

Little Johnny was nine years old and was watching a football game with his daddy one Sunday afternoon. His daddy popped open his fifth beer and Little Johnny said, "Daddy, can I have some beer?"

His daddy looked at him and said, "Johnny, does your wee wee reach your butt hole?"

Johnny looked confused and shook his head. "No."

"Then you can't have any beer."

A little while later Johnny's dad lit up a cigar. "Daddy," Johnny said, "Can I have a puff on your cigar?"

His daddy looked at him and said, "Johnny, does your wee wee reach your butt hole?"

Johnny looked up and said, "No."

"Then you can't smoke my cigar."

At halftime Johnny's dad realized he was out of beer, so he decided to walk down to the store on the corner and buy more. He asked Johnny if he wanted to go along. Johnny, of course, agreed to go. When they got to the store, Johnny's dad bought beer, cigars, and three lottery tickets. Johnny said, "Daddy, will you buy me a lottery ticket?"

Tired of saying no all day, Johnny's dad bought him a scratch-off lottery ticket. When Johnny scratched it off, he realized that it was worth $100,000.

Johnny's dad also realized it and said, "Johnny, think of how you can share that money with the rest of the family."

Johnny looked at his dad and said, "Daddy, does your wee wee reach your butt hole?"

Johnny's daddy said, "Why yes, Johnny, my wee wee does reach my butt hole."

"Good," Johnny said, "'Cuz you can go fuck yourself. This is my money."

8

Is It Possible To Be This Dumb? Part 2

Let's continue with some stories involving my wife. She was, for a number of years, the Principal of St. Augustine School, the Catholic School in Napoleon, Ohio. Before she was the Principal she was the 8th grade teacher. This meant that she went on every class trip for many years. The traditional class trip, taken every other year and involving the 7th and 8th graders and numerous parents, was to historic Williamsburg and to Washington DC.

One year my wife had a group of students numbering around twenty-five. She never had any trouble finding parents willing to ride the bus to Washington, and it was actually a good deal for her and the students, since the cost of the trip was based on forty-five seats on the bus.

Once the group got to the nation's capitol they got to tour numerous buildings and monuments. One of the buildings they got to tour was the Treasury Building. Since 9-11 security has been improved throughout the country, especially in major cities. Before going in to the Treasury Building everyone has to walk through a metal detector. One of the parents set off the buzzer on the metal detector.

The security officer asked him to go back through the metal detector and try again. Again the buzzer went off. They asked him to go back through and empty his pockets. He reached into his pocket and took out a Swiss army knife which was easily large enough to set off the alarm. However, as he removed the knife from his pocket he also pulled out a plastic bag of marijuana. Now think about how stupid this is. You not only try to enter a federal building with a knife, but you also have a bag of pot in the same pocket.

The parent was immediately arrested. My wife sent the rest of the group on the tour ahead and stayed with the parent until the police took him away. She never saw him again.

Another set of national
"Is It Possible To Be This Dumb?" incidents

1. A man was on trial in Pontiac, Michigan, and he claimed that he had been searched without a warrant. The prosecutor said the officer who arrested the man didn't need a warrant because of a "bulge" in the man's jacket made it seem reasonable to assume that he had a gun. "Nonsense," said the man who had been arrested. "This is the very jacket that I had on that day, and there's no bulge in it." The judge asked to see the jacket, and the man took it off and handed it over. When the judge discovered a large packet of cocaine in the jacket he laughed so hard he had to take a five minute recess.

2. A man in Oklahoma City was on trial for armed robbery of a convenience store. The store manager identified the man as the robber, at which the point the man yelled, "I should have blown your fucking head off." He paused, and then quickly added, ". . . if I had been the man who was there that night." The jury took 20 minutes to convict and recommend a 30-year sentence.

3. A guy walked into a liquor store one night to rob it. He demands all the cash in the store. As the worker is filling up a bag with the cash the robber spots a bottle of Crown Royal on the shelf. "And put that Crown Royal in the bag, too." The worker tells the robber that he can't give him the Crown Royal because he doesn't believe that he's 21. The robber takes out his driver's license to prove his age. Twenty minutes after he leaves the store he is arrested at home. The worker had memorized the address and had given it to the police.

4. A pair of Michigan robbers entered a record shop nervously waving revolvers. The first one shouted, "Nobody move." When his partner moved the startled bandit shot him!

9

A Legitimate Request

My wife was pregnant with our first son in September 1978 when she woke me up around 3:00 AM one Sunday morning. She told me her water had just broken. I jumped to my feet, grabbed some clothes, got dressed, and said, "OK, I'm ready. Let's go."

My wife looked at me like I was nuts.

"What's wrong?" I asked. "Are you ready to go?"

"It doesn't always work that way," she explained. "I haven't even started any contractions yet, but I just thought I better tell you that my water broke."

I was rarin' to go. I slept the rest of the night on top of the sheets and blankets in my clothes so that I would be ready to go when it was time. I took my wife to the hospital around 7:00 AM. She was examined by a nurse who told her to return home and stay comfortable, but that today was the day.

We returned home, had breakfast, relaxed (she may have relaxed, but I was too tense!). The Cleveland Browns were playing a home game against the San Diego Chargers that day, and I was really into the game. Her contractions started. It was a great game. The contractions got more intense and closer together. The Browns were driving.

With about two minutes to go in the first half I looked over at my wife. She was crumpled into the corner of the couch in obvious discomfort. She was trying to control her breathing and I was trying to cheer the Browns to a touchdown.

Jane finally looked over at me and said, in very real pain, "Stephen. Do you think we could go back to the hospital at halftime?"

"Of course we can," I said. For all of you out there who think I'm a real cad for waiting that long, let the record show that I did NOT wait until halftime to take my wife to the hospital to have our first child. I turned the television off and took her to the hospital one minute and eighteen seconds before the half. Right after the Browns scored a touchdown to take the lead.

Our son was born at 8:11 PM that night.

A Few Classic Irish Jokes

This first joke is one of Conor Flannary's favorites. I wish I could remember the first time I heard it, but I hear it every time we are together and dates and times sometimes get jumbled.

A group of Irish women were harvesting potatoes in their gardens. One of them, Brigitte Mary, picked up a potato and rubbed it for a few seconds. Everyone else was looking at her. She finally said, somewhat embarrassed, "Aye, this feels just like me Shawn's testicles."

"Oooh, that large, aye?" said one of the other ladies.

"Nah," said Brigitte Mary, "That dirty."

One day an Irish farmer was digging in his field when he hit something hard. He dug around it and finally pulled out an old vase. As he started wiping it off, a leprechaun appeared. "Yah finally dug me up and saved me," snarled the leprechaun. "Now be quick with yah. I'm old and tired and I've only got one gift left to give. What'll it be that you'll be wanting?"

The Irish farmer thought for a second and said. "Golly, I really don't know. I've got all the land I want. Me crops are growing well. Me animals are all healthy and I've got a great and loving wife. I really am not in need of anything."

The leprechaun was already getting impatient. "I'll ask ye again. What'll it be that you'll be wanting?"

The man thought some more and finally said, "How about this? Every time I take a piss the piss turns into the greatest tasting Irish whiskey known ta man. Can ye do that for me?"

The leprechaun snapped his fingers and disappeared.

Late that afternoon the man returned to his house from the field. "Molly," he called to his wife. "Bring me an old, clean jar." Molly brought the jar out and was horrified when the farmer peed into the jar, almost filling it.

"Why Seamus," said the wife. "What on earth are ye doin'?" The farmer explained the incident with the leprechaun. He looked at the liquid in the jar. It looked like Irish whiskey. He smelled the liquid in the jar. It smelled like Irish whiskey. With great hesitation he actually took a sip. It tasted like wonderful Irish whiskey!

Every day he would come home from the field and his wife would bring out two jars. He would pee into both bottles and give one to his wife and keep one for himself. They enjoyed this "cocktail" for many months.

One day he came home from the field and only peed into one jar. "What's the story, Seamus? What're ye doin'?"

Seamus just nodded his head for a second and said, "C'mere Molly. Today, me wife, ya get to learn ta drink from the bottle."

10

He Really Had To Pee

The wonder of childbirth is incredible. When we had our first child (of all the times to reconsider the use of the word "our," childbirth might be number one. I was there, but my wife did all the work!) I was in constant wonder in the delivery room. It was so exciting that I never even got grossed out. Hey, if you've ever been in a delivery room, birth definitely CAN be considered gross by some people.

Anyway, during the birth of our first son it was so interesting and exciting I never got grossed out or light-headed at all. I was too wrapped up in the entire process, and I was too busy trying to comfort my wife. The second son was completely different. I was clearly light-headed and grossed out at times. I even left the room a few times to catch my breath.

When our son was finally born, there were a few hectic moments. The doctor and the nurses really jumped to attention when they noticed the umbilical cord was wrapped around our son's neck. The professionals really worked quickly and hard to get the cord unwrapped and get our son breathing.

It seemed like as soon as they got the cord unwrapped and our son started breathing he also started peeing. The doctor held him up and his little penis was firing a stream of pee all around the room. The doctor couldn't control the aim, and our son peed for a long, long time. It was as if he came out and said, "I've had four beers and three cups of coffee and I'm gonna explode if I don't get rid of some of this!"

He really did pee for a long time, and I couldn't believe how far the little guy could shoot that stream!

Really Pissed Off

We've all had strange dates, but this one really takes the cake. Heard a story the other day that was supposed to have been on The Tonight Show. Supposedly, Jay Leno went into the audience to ask about the most embarrassing date anyone ever had. Here's what I heard . . . .

It was the middle of winter and a girl agreed to go on a date with a guy she had known for awhile but had never dated. They were going to go skiing, and return the same evening. Everything went fine during the day, and they actually had a nice time hitting the slopes.

Early in the evening they were headed home when the girl realized that she should not have had the third cup of coffee in the lodge. She really had to pee! Her date suggested, since they were headed down the mountain with really nowhere to stop, that she hold it. She did for awhile, but she eventually insisted that she had to stop. She convinced her date that she would stop and pee by the roadside, but she just had to pee. She basically told him to stop or she would pee all over his front seat.

He stopped the car and she quickly got out. She was slipping and sliding around in the deep snow, so once she got her pants down she sat back against the rear fender to steady herself. Her date was truly gallant and stood on the side of the car watching for traffic and not peeking. All she could think of was the relief she felt despite the rather embarrassing situation.

Upon finishing, the young lady soon became aware of another sensation. As she tried to stand to pull up her pants, she realized that her buttocks were frozen to the bumper of the car. Thoughts of tongues frozen to poles came to her mind immediately as she tugged away.

Her date finally called over, "What's taking so long?"

She replied, appropriately, "I'm freezing my butt off and I need some assistance."

The guy came around the car and she tried to cover herself with her sweater. Being the guy that he was, he burst out laughing. She, too, got the giggles, and they finally composed themselves and tried to figure out what to do. They both knew that it would take something hot to free her cheeks from the icy metal.

Thinking about what had gotten her into the predicament in the first place, they both quickly realized that there was only one way to get her free. This time she was the one who had to look away, as he unzipped his pants, took out his unit, and peed her butt off of the bumper.

This incident certainly gives a new meaning to the term "pissed off."

BE 03-01-04

Daddy's Really Special

A mother had just told her daughter all about making babies. Little Susie was sitting there quietly, but she had a look of confusion on her face.

"Do you understand it now?" asked her mother.

"Yes, I think so."

The mother then asked, "Do you have any other questions?"

"Well, sort of," said the little girl. "How about kitties? How does that work?"

"It works exactly the same way as babies."

The little girl's eyes got big. "Wow," she said. "My daddy can do anything!"

11

"Why Mrs. Francis, You Don't . . ."

Perhaps this section could have been included in the 'college' section, but it really deals with my mother, so I have included it in the 'family' section.

One day when I was a junior in college and living in the fraternity house, a fraternity brother came to me and asked me if there was any way I could take him to the airport in Cleveland. He knew that I didn't have classes the next day and he knew that I was from the Cleveland area. I told him that I would be happy to take him to the airport, but that I would need to use his car because I wasn't sure if my car, "Old Blue," would make it that far without breaking down. My fraternity brother had on old Volkswagon Beetle, but it ran pretty well.

Next, I went to my best friend, Bill Klein, and asked him if he wanted to go with us. He said he would go along. He then invited another fraternity brother, Lenny Rivers. Hell, now it was a Road Trip! My parents and my sister lived in Lorain, Ohio, which is on the way back from the Cleveland airport. I called my mother and asked her if I could bring two guys with me for dinner and to spend the night. I wanted to show my fraternity brothers where I lived and a few of the bars in the Lorain area. My mother not only said that it would be fine to bring the guys home, but she also promised to hold dinner for us as long as she knew approximately when we would arrive.

We drove our fraternity brother to the airport, never parked his car, but dropped him at the curb so we could make dinner by 7:00 at my parents' house. My fifteen-year-old sister Julia was still living at home and she joined us for dinner.

My family always ate dinner in the formal dining room, and that night was no exception. We used cloth napkins every night, and we had to be cleaned up and dressed right for dinner. Dinner was a pretty formal event.

I don't remember what we had to eat that night, but I'm sure it was good. When the dishes were cleared we had dessert. After dessert my mother looked at Bill and Lenny and said, "If you guys want to smoke, go ahead."

Lenny pulled out a pack of Salems, Bill pulled out some Newports, and my mother took out a pack of Kools. In case you aren't aware, all three of those brands are menthol cigarettes. All three of them lit up and started puffing away.

There were a few moments of silence while they smoked and my father had his coffee, when, out of the clear blue, my mother said, "Did you guys ever notice that all young people who smoke marijuana also smoke menthol cigarettes?"

Where in the hell did that come from? First of all, where did my mother ever come up with that idea?

Within three very, very long seconds, all eyes at the table had looked at the three packs of cigarettes. All were menthol. Silence. Awkward silence. Bill broke the silence by saying, "Why Mrs. Francis, you don't smoke marijuana do you?"

I absolutely couldn't believe that he asked that question to my mother. She looked down at the packs of menthol cigarettes and then said, while laughing, "Oh, no, no, no. I don't smoke marijuana." Everybody laughed. Rather uneasy laughs for some of the people at the table, but laughs nonetheless. It really would have been interesting if she had asked Bill that same question.

Huh? Some Jokes For My Mother

My mother is a remarkable person. She did an incredible job keeping our family together through some mighty tough times. She has worn a hearing aid since I can remember, so if you think the first few of these jokes are making fun of hearing-impaired people, please consider that I grew up in a home with someone who was hearing impaired, so I feel I can tell these.

Three older women walking down the street one day. The first one says, "It's windy today, isn't it?"

The second one says, "No it's not. It's Thursday."

The third one says, "So am I. Let's go get a cup of coffee."

The same three women arrive at the coffee shop. The first one says to the second one, "Ethel, I understand you got a new hearing aid."

"That's right," says Ethel.

"What kind is it?" asks the first woman.

Ethel looks at her wrist and says, "It's around a quarter to three."

Now they sit down and order their coffee. The first lady says, "It's terrible getting old. Why the other day I opened the refrigerator and couldn't remember whether I was getting something out or putting something away."

The second lady says, "Oh, I had something like that happen just the other day. I stopped on the landing of the stairs to straighten a picture hanging there and then I couldn't remember whether I was going up the stairs or down the stairs."

The third lady says, "I've really been lucky. I haven't had anything like that happen to me, knock on wood." She wraps her knuckles on the table, stands up, looks at the others and says, "Stay seated, I'll get the door."

12

A Near-Serious Case Of Mistaken Identity

This next incident could be included in the college section of this book, but I chose to include it here because, well, I don't know other than to say it really is about me and I'm part of that strange family.

Before a student can student-teach, he/she must go through a lengthy "Field Experience/Observation." That's what they used to call it at Defiance College, but I suppose they have a new name for it by now. Pre-Student Teaching, Methods, whatever. College students have to spend a certain amount of time in a classroom to determine if they really want to student teach and then head into the teaching profession. In 1973 we had to spend ten days in a classroom setting for this pre-student teaching experience. I believe students now have to spend an entire semester, but back then it was ten days in a classroom.

Defiance College used to have a 4-1-4 program, which meant that students would take four classes fall semester, one class winter term (January), and four classes spring semester. The winter term allowed students to travel, focus on unusual-and-still-academic topics and classes, etc. For example, members of the speech team were often on campus all through January and focused on preparing competitive speeches all day, every day. Every year a group of students would travel to Europe, and every year a group of instructors and students would travel to Arizona for archeological digs.

My freshman year I enrolled in a winter term class called "History of The Cinema." We went in every day and watched an old movie and then talked about it. Some days we had a morning movie and afternoon movie. Mostly, I went to the gym and played basketball. My sophomore year I did the speech team thing, where I practiced my competitive speeches all day, every day and then competed at speech tournaments around the country.

My junior year I enrolled in "Educational Field Experience/Observation." I was going to spend the winter term at home while visiting my alma mater, Lorain Catholic High School. I was supposed to observe different teachers and their techniques, teaching methods, blah, blah, blah. I had made all of the arrangements with the Principal, Sister Mary Neumann. Sister Mary Neumann was a great lady. She was the Principal in the last two years of St. Mary's Academy, and she was the first Principal at Lorain Catholic. She knew me very well and quickly agreed to let me do this field experience at LC.

I arrived the first morning around 8:20. I think school started at 8:05, but I was just this college kid coming to observe teachers, so my being late shouldn't have been too big a deal. Sister Mary Neumann met me at the door and said, "Stephen Francis, it is so good to see you. Welcome home. You will substituting for Mrs. Havrady today."

I looked at her and stopped in my tracks. "What?" I asked. I was supposed to just sit around, maybe run off some papers, maybe even grade a few papers, but substitute? I was not ready for this, either emotionally or mentally.

"Oh, I know you're not supposed to teach yet, but Mrs. Havrady called in sick and you can handle it. She's an English teacher and you're going to be an English teacher, so you can handle it." Sister Mary Neumann walked me down to Room 102 D. She walked me to the front of the room, handed me some lesson plans, and introduced me to the students. I was a bit in shock, and students can spot a "newbie" from a mile away. I somehow managed to get through the first period, but I was really struggling.

At the end of the period a very attractive blonde teacher stuck her head around the corner into my room and said, "Hi, I'm Karen Mislinski. I teach in Room 102 C, and if you have any trouble today just let me know and I'll help you out." The day was suddenly looking up.

I made sure that I had numerous questions for my new friend. She looked to be about twenty-five years old. She had medium-length blonde hair with fine, fair features. She also had a very engaging smile. She also didn't wear a wedding ring. Yep, I suddenly had questions at the end of each class period.

As the week progressed I worked with numerous other teachers, but I always made sure that I had seventh period free. You see, seventh period was also Karen Mislinski's free period, and I still had plenty of questions. I don't know about most people, but I have always been a little shy about asking someone out. Most people I know would never agree with me being shy about anything, but when I was twenty years old asking someone you just met a day or two earlier in a professional setting was going to take some time, patience, and courage.

Each day that week I talked to Karen more and more. I was breaking the ice, and I was just about ready to ask her out for a beer after school. I also got the impression that Karen enjoyed spending time with me.

On Friday of that week I made sure I had seventh period free, and I knew where I could find Karen Mislinski. She usually grabbed a cup of tea and headed for the English Department Office. Sure enough, when I got enough courage I went in to the office and started some small talk. I was right on the verge of saying, in my absolutely coolest voice (which wasn't very cool at all), "So, Karen, interested in going out for a beer after school today?"

I mean I was just about getting those words out when a student knocked on the door. Karen said, "Come in."

The student stepped into the office and said, "I'm sorry to bother you Sister, but I'm looking for Coach Englund. Have you seen him?"

I think I got my first case of whiplash as my head spun around. I felt like the little girl in "The Exorcist!" The student had called my dearest Karen "Sister." As in NUN. After Karen told the student that she hadn't seen Coach Englund, she looked back at me. I don't think I hid my surprise very well. Karen just looked at me for a second, smiled that great smile, and said, "What's wrong? I think you were going to ask me something."

I sat there dumbfounded. It took a second or two, but I eventually just pointed to the door and mumbled, "That . . . student . . . called . . . you . . . Sister."

"Well, yes," smiled Karen. "I'm Sister Karen Mislinski, IHM." That meant she was a nun in the order of The Sisters And Servants of the Immaculate Heart Of Mary. She was a nun!!!! I was five seconds away from asking a nun out for a beer! That's not fair! Nuns were supposed to wear the long robes and habits. Hey, nuns were definitely not supposed to look like Karen Mislinski! In my head I immediately thought to call her Sister Mary What-a-waste.

The darnedest thing about this story is that I'm actually pretty confident that Karen Mislinski would have gone out after school with me for a beer. Of course I never would have asked her if I had known she was a nun. Hell, I never did ask her when I found out she was a nun. That's just not fair.

Oooh, here's a scary thought. What if that student hadn't interrupted us? What if I had asked Karen Mislinski out for a beer not knowing that she was a nun? What if she had gone? What if I asked her later if she wanted to go parking at Lakeview? Now THAT would have been an interesting time to find out she was a nun. It was clearly better that I found out when I did. I think it saved both of us some embarrassment.

Son Of A Bitch Fish

The parish priest went on a fishing trip. On the last day of his trip he hooked a monster fish and reeled it in. The guide, holding a net, yelled, "Look at the size of that son of a bitch!"

The priest said, "Excuse me, but I'm a priest and I would prefer that you not use language like that."

"No father," said the guide. "That's what kind of fish it is. It's a Son of a Bitch fish."

"Really? Well, then help me reel in this Son of a Bitch."

Once in the boat they marveled at the size of the fish. "Father, that's the largest Son of a Bitch I've ever seen."

"Yes," said the priest. "It certainly is a big Son of a Bitch. What should I do with it?"

"Why father, eat it of course. That Son of a Bitch will taste great."

The priest took the fish home with him to the rectory. While unloading his gear and his prize catch, Sister Mary Elizabeth inquired about his trip. "Take a look at this Son of a Bitch," said the priest.

The nun grabbed the rosary around her throat and protested, "Father! Such language."

"It's OK sister, that's the kind of fish it is. It's called a Son of a Bitch fish."

"Really," said the nun. "Well, what are you going to do with that Son of a Bitch?"

"Why eat it, of course. The fishing guide told me that nothing tastes better than a Son of a Bitch."

Sister Mary Elizabeth told the priest that the new bishop had scheduled a parish visit for the next day and she suggested they fix the fish for his dinner. "I'll even clean the Son of a Bitch," she said.

As she was cleaning the fish the friar walked in. "What are you doing, sister?"

"Father wants me to clean this Son of a Bitch for the bishop's dinner."

"Sister! I'll clean it if you're that upset."

"No, no, no. That's the kind of fish it is."

"Really? Well, in that case I'll fix a great meal to go with it," said the Friar.

On the night of the bishop's visit, everything was perfect. The Friar had prepared an excellent meal. The wine was fine and the fish was excellent. The new bishop was very pleased with the meal and said, "This is great fish. Where did you get it?"

"I caught the Son of a Bitch," proclaimed the proud priest.

"And I cleaned the Son of a Bitch," exclaimed the nun.

The bishop sat in silent disbelief.

The Friar added, "And I prepared the Son of a Bitch using one of my special recipes."

The new bishop looked around at each of them. Slowly, a big smile crept across his face as he said, "You know what? You fuckers are my kind of people."

Section II

If High School Was Incredibly Funny . . . .

13

The Incomparable Bill Rousch

The custodian at St. Mary's Academy in Lorain, Ohio, was a cranky, old difficult-to-like-but-easy-to-love guy named Bill Rousch. He had been the custodian at St. Mary's for years and years, and was just about as powerful around the place as Monsignor James J. Duffy.

I asked Bill one day how old he was. He growled at me, "Seventeen." I just laughed and said, "Really, how old are you?"

"Seventeen," he insisted.

"I don't get it," I said. "What do you mean by that?"

"Listen, kid," he said. "I've only celebrated seventeen birthdays in my whole goddamn life. I swear I've only had seventeen birthdays. I'll have my eighteenth birthday next year."

I left him thinking that the old guy had finally lost it completely. I found out later that Bill was actually 71 years old. He was born on February 29, so on his last birthday (number seventeen) he was actually 68 years old. He wasn't lying when he told me that he had only celebrated seventeen birthdays.

My brother Jack and I used to sneak into the gym whenever we possibly could to play basketball. There were about a dozen guys who would figure out a way to sneak in to play whenever we didn't have school, weekend afternoons, etc. Dozens of times we would be in the middle of a game when Bill Rousch would storm in the gym and begin to yell and wave his arms. He always said the same thing.

"What the hell's goin' on in here? Get the hell oughta here. Get oughta this goddamn gym!"

My brother Jack and his friends used to love to torture Bill Rousch. The boiler room was also his office, and it contained some furniture, a phone, a desk, and all sorts of tools. The phone was really the only reason any of us ever went down to the boiler room. If we needed a ride home after practice (or after getting kicked out of the gym) we could always go to the boiler room and use the phone in there.

There was also an air vent from the hallway steps which opened directly into the boiler room. The vent actually covered an exhaust fan and was covered with a grate, but it was right above Bill's desk. My brother and his friends would check to see if Bill was sitting in his boiler room and then they would use these creepy voices through the vent.

"Biiilllll. Biiiilllll. Biiiilllll Rousch," they would chant through the grated vent. The fan really added a great sound to their voices. It really creeped the old guy out, and he finally told somebody that he thought the school was haunted because he kept hearing these voices.

I didn't actually hear the next line from Bill Rousch's mouth, but it has been related to me many times by Fred Knillen, a student in the class of 1969. When St. Mary's added Johnston Hall in the late 1950's they added a downstairs cafeteria and Home Economics room, a gym on the main floor, and a library on the top floor. During the winter the library was always very cold, since it was the farthest room in the building from the boilers.

One particularly cold day Sister Rita, who was the librarian, sent Fred Knillen from the library down to tell Bill Rousch that the library was very cold and needed some heat. Fred went down to the boiler room and Bill was sitting on his recliner.

"Hey Bill," started Knillen. "Sister Rita sent me down to tell you that the library is really cold today."

"Oh yeah," grumbled the custodian. "Tell her to burn some of the goddamn books. Nobody reads the goddamn things anyway."

I don't think that Fred Knillen went up and told Sister Rita what Bill had said, however true it actually was.

Sister Maria Confesses

Throughout this book there will be various "topics" about which I know some jokes. I first heard this joke in the spring of 1973 at an Iota Phi Chapter of Tau Kappa Epsilon "Hell Night." Hell Night is supposed to be very serious, but, just like Rush Parties, guys seemed to always have a few jokes ready for the evening. It should be pointed out that I heard almost the exact version of the joke in March 2007 on the way to a Cleveland Indians Spring Training game in Winter Haven, Florida. Later in the week I received another version of the same joke via e-mail from my sister Veronica. Isn't it interesting how jokes just keep floating around the planet?

Sister Maria returned to the convent one afternoon and immediately went to see Sister Frederica, the straight-laced, veteran Mother Superior of the convent.

"Reverend Mother, I am looking for Father Kelly. I need to make a confession," said the young nun.

"I'm sorry, Sister," said the Mother Superior, "but Father Kelly is gone to see his Aunt in Colorado for three days. Perhaps I can hear your confession."

"Well, alright," said the young nun. "Bless me for I have sinned. I used some terrible language while golfing today. On the fourth hole I hit a career drive about 225 yards right down the middle of the fairway. As I was walking to my ball a squirrel ran out of the woods and picked my ball up in its mouth."

"And that's when you used the bad language?"

"No Sister, please let me finish. The squirrel was running back towards the woods with my ball in its mouth when a large hawk swooped out of the sky and snatched up the squirrel with my ball still in its mouth."

"Oh, I see. That's when you used the bad language?"

"No Sister. As the hawk was flying away with the squirrel and my ball, the squirrel dropped the ball out of its mouth right near the green and into the sand trap."

"Ahh," said the older nun. "That is when you used the bad language, right?"

"Please let me finish. My ball was dropped from quite high, and it hit a rake in the sand trap and bounced onto the green and rolled down the green to just over two feet from the pin."

"Don't tell me," said the Mother Superior, "You missed the fucking putt!"

The Mother Superior Calls . . . .

The Mother Superior calls all the nuns into a meeting and says, "I have something very important to tell you. We have a case of Gonorrhea in our convent."

In the back of the room an old nun calls out, "Thank God. I'm really getting tired of that white zinfandel."

14

It It Possible To Be This Dumb? Part 3

I'm sure that young people have always been very daring. A lot of people might call daring just plain dumb. In the sixties and seventies there seemed to be lots of young people (almost all guys) willing to race cars on public streets. I can honestly say that I was never driving during a drag race or any other kind of race on a public street, but that doesn't mean I wasn't a passenger a few times. One time in particular answers the question asked at the beginning of this chapter.

There was a place on the west side of Lorain that we all called "The Salt Flats." We named it after The Bonneville Salt Flats in Utah, which is the site of just every attempt to set a land speed record. Our Salt Flats was simply a neighborhood that never was. What I mean by this is some developer poured streets for a neighborhood, but then never built any houses. He probably ran out of money after putting in the sewers, roads, etc. Thus, there were these beautiful blacktop streets with no houses anywhere around. Needless to say, beautiful, barren streets invite all sorts of racing.

None of the blocks were really long enough to drag race on, but they were perfect for racing around a block or two. Heck, it was like we had our own Indianapolis Motor Speedway.

One Sunday afternoon I was with Bert Knouwer (he was the first kid in the class with a driver's license) and Patsy Conrad and we were going to race around one of the blocks. We decided to use a "Le Mans start," which meant we would be out of the car, run to the car, start it, and see how long it would take us to make one lap around the block.

We started about twenty-five yards from the car, Bert's 1960 Corvair. Bert said, "Gentlemen. On your marks. Get set. Go." We sprinted to his car. I dove in the back seat while Bert and Patsy got into the front seat. Bert started the car, which, as I recall, was a three-speed manual transmission. Seat belts? Out of the question. Hell, I'm not sure the Corvair was even equipped with seat belts in the front, and I know there were no seat belts in the back.

Once the car was started Bert peeled out onto the road and we were off. We took the first turn at about twenty miles an hour, the second at about thirty. It was the third turn where things got scary. Bert took the 90 degree turn at around forty miles an hour, and the car left the road and started sliding on its side in the field. Needless to say, when we left the road and started to slide, the car slowed down pretty quickly. I do remember the car teetering on its side and almost turning over onto its top. I was straddled across the back seat, so I probably would have been OK, but Bert and Patsy might have been crushed had the car actually turned over on to its top.

That was one crazy afternoon, and I don't recall ever going to the Salt Flats after that to race cars. I know that many of my friends continued to do so.

One final set of "Is It Possible To Be This Dumb?" incidents

1. An unidentified man, using a shotgun like a club to break a former girlfriend's windshield, accidentally shot himself to death when the gun discharged, blowing a hole in his gut.

2. Police said a lawyer demonstrating the safety of windows in a downtown Toronto skyscraper crashed through a pane of glass with his shoulder and plunged 24 floors to his death. The lawyer was explaining the strength of the building's windows to visiting law students. The managing partner of the law firm called the young lawyer "one of our best and brightest" members of the 200-member firm.

3. A terrible diet and a room with no ventilation are being blamed for the death of a man who was killed by his own gas emissions. (See Chapter 3) There were no marks on his body, and an autopsy showed large amounts of methane gas in his system. His diet had consisted of beans and cabbage and a couple of other foods, which seemed to be the right combination. He died in his sleep from breathing the poisonous cloud that was hanging over his bed. When paramedics arrived, three of them got sick from the smell, and one was actually hospitalized.

4. Two local men were injured when their pickup truck left the road and struck a tree near Cotton Patch, Arkansas. Thurston Poole and Billy Ray Wallis were returning home after a frog gigging trip on an overcast Sunday night. Poole's pickup truck lost its headlights. The two men concluded that the headlight fuse on the older-model truck was burned out. As a replacement fuse was not available, Wallis noticed that a 22 caliber bullet from his pistol fit perfectly into the fuse box next to the steering wheel column. Upon inserting the bullet, the headlights again began to operate properly, and the two men proceeded eastbound toward White River Bridge.

After traveling approximately twenty miles, and just before crossing the river, the bullet apparently overheated, discharged, and struck Poole in the testicles. The vehicle swerved sharply to the right and struck a tree, injuring Wallis, who suffered a broken clavicle. Wallis had this to say: "Thank God we weren't on the bridge when Thurston shot his balls off, or we might both be dead."

The state trooper who investigated the accident said, "I've been a trooper for ten years, but this is a first for me. I can't believe those two would admit how the accident happened."

Upon being notified of the wreck, the driver's wife asked how many frogs the boys had caught.

15

The Look On Sister Elna's Face . . . .

One of the funniest things I ever witnessed was the look on Sister Elna's face in March 1966. Some background information is definitely needed on this one.

Sister Mary Elna was this small, slight, mean-spirited nun who taught seventh grade at St. Mary's Academy in Lorain, Ohio. Everyone called her "Hurricane Elna," not only because it was funny, but also because she could muster up quite a quick temper and she frequently lost control of herself. When her temper exploded she was a whirling dervish of out-of-control frenzy. The rumor was that she had been bitten by a rabid dog at one point in her life and never took shots for it. Older students passed down the story that they had actually seen her frothing at the mouth at times. She was scary for a five-foot-three, one-hundred-pound, seventy-year-old woman.

My two older brothers, Bob and Jack, had been students in Hurricane Elna's class before I got there, and she hated both of them. I could understand why she hated Jack, he was a wise guy who was in trouble all the time. On the very first day of seventh grade Sister Elna was calling the roll when she got to my name.

"Stephen Francis," she called out.

With my innocent, dimple-filled smile I raised my hand and said, "That's me, Sister."

She looked up over the edge of her glasses and asked, "Are you related to Bob and Jack Francis?"

"Why yes, Sister," I said. "They're my brothers."

She flashed me the first of many evil eyes. "I'll be watching YOU this year," she promised.

Shortly into the school year there was a bee flying around the room. We get those bees in the Midwest from August to October, and if you leave a pop can open you are liable to swallow a bee on your next sip. Anyway, there was a bee flying around and I reached up to swat it with an open hand. Just as I did, Jacqueline Plato, a girl sitting across the aisle from me, also reached out to swat it. Our hands clapped against each other making a pretty loud sound. Hurricane Elna was writing something on the board. She spun around and glared at me.

"What do you think you're doing back there Stephen Francis?"

"Well, Sister, there was this bee flying around and I tried to swat it . . . ."

"Don't you dare talk back to me," she screamed.

"If you didn't want me to answer you then why'd you ask me a question," I said. Oops. Mistake. Big mistake. She lost it. She grabbed a yardstick from behind her desk and came after me. It wasn't one of those quarter-inch flimsy things, either. This was one of those three-quarter inch meter sticks, a virtual weapon.

I wasn't going to sit there and be beat upon by a little old lady, so I got up from my desk as she rushed to me. She got within range and took a swing, which I easily managed to avoid. I started running from her, up and down the rows. I might also point out that we had 48 students in our seventh grade class, so Hurricane Elna was indeed making contact with people, just not me. I managed to stay far enough away from her until she got tired, which was actually longer than you might think. She eventually sent me to the office to face our principal, Mother Mary Donald.

That incident in seventh grade leads up to "The Look" from Hurricane Elna that was so priceless. In eighth grade our teacher was Sister Jacinta, but our class effectively drove her out of the school and into therapy. She was replaced by a full-time substitute named Mrs. Edna Gruelich. That was actually her name. Edna Gruelich. Can you imagine what a person named Edna Gruelich might look like? There, you have it. That's what she looked like. She was the first person I can recall who wore her glasses on a chain around her neck. Anyway, Mrs. Gruelich taught us every subject during the day except Religion, which had to be taught by a priest or a nun. Well, guess who was brought in as our eighth grade Religion teacher? That's right, Hurricane Elna. I thought I was finished with her for good, and, with a great deal of practice, patience, and prayer I had almost overcome my nightmares. Here she was, back in my waking and sleeping thoughts.

Everything was fine until one day I was passing a note to a girl I liked. I didn't realize it at the time, but most teachers have super-sonic hearing, and Hurricane Elna was one of those. Linda Cole sat three rows away from me, so I had to pass the note to Patsy Conrad. He passed it to Margaret Hernandez, and she passed it to Linda.

I wrote the note, went "Psst," to Patsy. He reached out his hand, took the note, and went "Psst," to Margaret, who did the same to hand the note to Linda. Linda answered the note and started the chain of "Psst's" to get the note back to me.

Hurricane Elna was in the front of the room and could faintly hear the "Psst's." When the note returned to me I quickly answered it and started the chain again. This time, however, Hurricane Elna heard me when I tried to hand it back to Patsy. She spun around to catch me in mid-act. Patsy Conrad had been facing the front of the room watching the teacher, and when he saw her turn around he took my hand instead of the note. So here we were, two eighth-grade boys holding hands in the back of the room. Hurricane Elna had a great view. She was looking right down the aisle at Patsy holding my hand and swinging it. She did the classic double-take and continued to stare. For the briefest of moments I didn't know what Patsy was doing when he took my hand, but I slowly turned and looked forward, only to see Hurricane Elna staring at us. I tilted my head just a bit and gave her the sweetest smile I could muster.

There it was! The look on her face was incredible. She sort of twisted her face into a strange contortion. The rest of the class watched her, staring and frozen, for a few seconds and wondered what the hell was going on. Someone told me later that they thought she might have had a stroke. Patsy and I knew what was going on, but no one else did.

Do you know what she eventually did? Nothing. She stood there with that look on her face for awhile and then went on with the lesson. No one had ever taught her how to respond to two eighth-grade boys holding hands in the back of the room. She had no idea what to do, so she did nothing.

I know that I will never forget that look on her face.

. . . . And Then The Nun Fainted

Little Mary was not the best student at St. Aloysius School. She was constantly falling asleep in class, especially Religion class, which happened to be the first period of the day. One day Sister Jacinta called on her to answer a question.

"Tell me, Mary, who created the universe?"

Little Johnny was sitting behind Mary and he poked her in the butt with his sharpened pencil. Mary woke up with a start and yelled, "God Almighty!"

"Very good," said Sister Jacinta.

A few minutes later Mary fell back asleep and sister Jacinta asked her, Who is our Lord and Savior?"

Again, Johnny poked her with the pencil. "Jesus Christ!" shouted Mary.

"Very good," said the nun.

A few minutes later the nun asked Mary a third question. "What did Eve say to Adam after they had their twenty-third child?"

Johnny poked Mary one more time and Mary woke up and said, "If you stick that thing in me one more time I swear I will break it in half."

Sister Jacinta fainted.

16

A Four-For-One Incident

See. Taste. Smell. Touch.

All four of those senses were involved in this next incident.

I was an eighth-grader at St. Mary's School in Lorain, Ohio, in the fall of 1965. At the very beginning of the school year, I believe it was the second day of school, I noticed my parents in the hallway of the school after the final bell for the day. I just assumed that my brother Jack was again in trouble. However, my parents, with three other sets of parents, came into my classroom after everyone else had left. The fearsome principal of the school, Mother Mary Donald, joined our teacher, Sister Jacinta, with the other parents and three of my classmates. I wondered what in the world was happening. It was, after all, only the second day of the school year, and I hadn't been in any trouble yet.

Mother Mary Donald started the conversation by pointing out that the four students present were some of the top students in the class. She explained that she had called the parents together to offer a unique program at St. Mary's School. The school had decided to allow the four of us to give up our lunch hour and recess time so that we could take a class up in the high school. All of the parents thought it was a brilliant idea and quite a compliment to us. Even my fellow classmates thought it was a good idea.

Whoa, I thought to myself. This is definitely NOT a good idea. Who wants to give up lunch and recess to take an extra class during the eighth-grade year? When you're in eighth grade you are the kings of the playground. It's your last chance to be a little kid. I had plans to mess around all year with my friends Mackie MacGregor and Conor Flanary. This was flat out wrong.

The principal explained that we could take either Algebra I or Latin I. My father jumped in with, "Stephen will take Latin I. I took four years of Latin while attending St. Mary's, you know," he said with a bit of pride. How could I stop this madness from happening?

I couldn't, and every day for the rest of the school year four eighth grade students left class at 11:05 and went to the cafeteria. There was no one else there, and we were allowed eight minutes to eat. We then had to go up to the third floor to the high school to take our Latin I class. It was horrible!

Obviously, I entered the class with a very poor attitude, and I thus learned very little. Oh, I earned a "B" in the class, which pleased my parents, but I learned very little.

The next school year, my freshman year, I was assigned to Latin II. Since I hadn't learned much in Latin I, Latin II was going to be a real struggle. Meanwhile, all of my friends were in Latin I class, taught that year by a first-year teacher named Mr. Rafsky. Mr. Rafsky had this whiny voice and had absolutely no control over the class. The class met third period, which happened to be the same period the freshmen girls all had Religion class. There were 20 freshmen boys in a class taught by a first-year teacher who had no idea what he was getting himself into. During that same third period I was assigned Study Hall, since I had already completed Latin I.

I heard some great stories about the shenanigans going on in Mr. Rafsky's third period Latin I class. The class behaved so poorly that Mother Mary Donald had to go to the classroom several times each day to settle down the students. Those guys were out of control. Once they realized that Mother Mary Donald was going to check on them every day during that period, they came up with a great plan. Someone would get Mr. Rafsky's attention on one side of the room and someone else would go and lock the door from the inside. There was frosted glass on the door, so you could see when someone was out there, you just couldn't tell who it was.

Every day Mother Mary Donald would go to check on the classroom, and every day she would try the door, find it locked, and then take out her keys, open the door, and walk in. During the time that it took her to take out her keys and open the door, everyone would rush back to his seat and sit there like he was behaving.

After about three weeks of listening to the stories of things going on in the room during that period, I figured I had to do something to get in there. One of my friends suggested that I just start skipping study hall. I couldn't get myself to do that, so I hatched another plan. I made an appointment with Mother Mary Donald. She was a large, scary nun. I figured she was about six-foot, one ninety, with one eyebrow all the way across. Whoosh. I went to her office and explained that I was really struggling in Latin II, that I had a Study Hall third period, there was a Latin I class that period, and I wondered if I might be able to sit in on the Latin I class as sort of a refresher. All I wanted, of course, was to be in the Latin I class with my buddies.

Mother Mary Donald agreed that it might be a good idea, so she completed paperwork for me to drop Study Hall and pick up Latin I. I went to the Latin I classroom, heard craziness going on inside, and tried the door. It was locked, so I knocked. It sounded like the room got very quiet. Mr. Rafsky answered the door and let me in. When my freshmen friends saw it was only me, it got crazy right away. Mr. Rafsky had to sign a slip allowing me in the class, and, as he did this, Gary James calmly walked past us and locked the door. It was just about that time that an eraser flew past our heads.

A week or so later Conor Flanary came into class and asked us all if we wanted to chew some tobacco that day. He had a large block of tobacco. It wasn't the loose stuff that became popular years later, but this was a chaw. It was a block of tobacco that you bit. You bit off as much as you wanted and that was how much you had in your mouth. Being the crazy freshmen that we were, most of us took a bite and started trying to chew.

The taste of that was disgusting! We didn't know what we were doing, so we were swallowing much of the juice. Terrible.

Gary James stood up and said, "Rafsky, I gotta go to the john." He left the classroom, unlocking the door. Moments later, Mother Mary Donald made her daily visit to the classroom. Most of us saw her huge, hulking figure outside the door as she came in and quickly reached up and took the chaws of tobacco into our hands. That was one disgusting feeling. Yuck.

Unfortunately, Conor Flanary was turned around talking to us when Mother Mary Donald entered the room, so he didn't see her. He saw us take out the tobacco and hold it in our hands. He slowly turned around and looked up at this frightening nun staring at him from just a few feet away. He looked up at her and, gulp, swallowed his whole chaw of tobacco. I almost threw up right then thinking about it. She stayed in the room and yelled at us for awhile. We were sitting right behind Conor, and we watched as he turned green and his head started rolling from side to side. That was one funny sight.

Moments after Mother Mary Donald left Conor got up and started running to the restroom. He at least hoped to make it to the drinking fountain. He didn't make it. He threw up in his hands on the way to the restroom. Again, disgusting. But that's not the worst. I told you there were four senses involved in this story. When he returned and told us that he had thrown up in his hands, he asked us if we wanted to smell his hands. He hadn't washed them. Yep. Some of us actually took a whiff of those hands. Our senses of taste, sight, touch, and smell would never be the same.

Little Johnny On Getting Older

When we get together, everyone is supposed to bring jokes to tell. Too often we tell the same jokes over and over, and, quite honestly, some of the best jokes deserved to be told over and over. Here's one told around a fire in Bill Klein's beautiful backyard in Solon:

Little Johnny was sitting at a park bench munching on one candy bar after another. After the sixth candy bar a man looked over at him and said, "Son, you know eating all that candy can't be good for you. It will give you acne, rot your teeth, and eventually make you fat." Johnny looked at the man and said, "My grandfather lived to be 94 years old."

"Really," inquired the stranger. "Did he eat six candy bars at a time?"

"No," replied little Johnny, "he minded his own fucking business."

Little Johnny At School

One day the teacher says to the class, "Today we are going to talk about Life's Little Lessons. Does anyone have a story about a life lesson that he or she might share with the class?"

Suzie raises her hand and says, "My Aunt Jane and Uncle Frank live on a farm. They sell eggs to the local market. One week last summer I got to spend time at their farm. Every morning we would get up and go check the chicken coop and collect the eggs that had been laid. We put the eggs into this big basket and then took them to the market. We were sitting in the front of the truck and I got to hold the basket with the eggs. They have a long driveway at their farm, and it has a bunch of holes and ruts. They let me sit in the middle of them and hold the basket. My Uncle Frank was driving, and he hit a rut. The basket sort of popped up in the air and then so did some of the eggs. When they landed they broke all over the other eggs."

"And what was the lesson that you learned?" asked the teacher.

"Why, that's easy," said little Suzie. "Don't put all your eggs in one basket."

"That's very good, Suzie. Does anyone else have a story?"

Bobby raised his hand. "I have one. My Aunt Mary and Uncle Mike have a farm too, and they raise chickens. Last summer I got to spend a week with them. One day we went out and all the chickens had laid an egg. We were going to collect the eggs, but I asked my Aunt Mary if we could let some of them go and have the hens hatch the eggs so I'd have some chicks to take home. She told me yes and she told me to go out and count the ones that we wouldn't touch. I counted fourteen eggs that we didn't collect. That night a fox got in the henhouse and broke all the eggs."

"And what lesson did you learn that day?" asked the teacher.

"Why that's easy," said Bobby. "Don't count your chickens before they're hatched."

"That's very good," said the teacher. "Anyone else?"

Little Johnny raised his hand and said, "I've got one. I have an Uncle Vince who fought in the Vietnam War. He used to fly fighter planes. One time he was over enemy territory and he got shot out of the sky. He hit his ejector seat and left the crashing plane. He pulled is ripcord for his parachute and was floating to the ground. All he had with him was a gun, a big knife, and a bottle of whiskey. As he was floating down he decided that he might as well chug the bottle of whiskey, since he was going to be landing behind enemy lines, so he chugged the bottle of whiskey. When he landed, he was attacked by a bunch of Vietnamese, and he shot a whole bunch of them. When he ran out of bullets he killed the rest of them with his knife."

There was a pause before the teacher asked, "And what lesson are we supposed to learn from that story?"

"Oh," Johnny said. "This is an important lesson that my dad says all the time. Don't fuck with Uncle Vince when he's been drinking."

Little Johnny came home from school one day and told his dad that he got an "F" in math.

"Why?" asked the father."

"Well, the teacher asked me 'How much is 2 X 3?' I said, 'Six.'"

"But that's the right answer," complained the dad.

"Yeah, but then she said, 'How much is 3 X 2?'"

"What's the fucking difference?" asked the father.

"That's exactly what I said!"

One day the teacher said, "Today we are going to learn multi-syllabic words." Does anyone have an example of a multi-syllabic word?"

Johnny raised his hand and said, "I do. Masturbate."

The teacher was a bit flustered and said, "Wow, Johnny. That's a mouthful."

Little Johnny shook his head and said, "Uh-uh, teacher. That would be a blow-job, but it's nice to know you're thinking about that."

The teacher said that the class was going to work on grammar. "I would like everyone to think of an example when you heard the word *beautiful*."

Suzie raised her hand and said, "My father bought my mother some flowers and she said to him, 'Hank, these flowers are beautiful.'"

"Very good, Suzie," the teacher said. "Anyone else?"

Michael raised his hand and said, "My mommy planned a beautiful dinner and it came out beautifully."

"That's also very good," said the teacher. Johnny raised his hand and the teacher reluctantly called on him, thinking 'How can he mess up using the word beautiful?'

Johnny said, "Last night at dinner my sister told my father that she was pregnant. He looked across the table and said, 'That's beautiful, just fucking beautiful.'"

17

Mackie Is Always Thinking

This story just occurred a few years ago, but I think it needs to be included in the high school section, since it actually occurred way back in the early '70's.

A couple of years ago we were sitting around after a golf outing and Mackie MacGregor looked at Coach Englund and said, with all seriousness, "I have a serious question. Second semester of my sophomore year I got an "F" in Religion class from Father Penny. Since he's no longer a priest (Father Penny left the priesthood and married a nun we used to call Sister Mini-skirt), can I have that Religion grade expunged? I think that would raise my grade point average up over a two point."

We all thought that was funny as hell. How long had he been thinking of that? Where does he come up with these things?

More Irish Jokes

We all love Irish jokes, and Conor Flannary seemed to come up with more Irish jokes than anyone else. Here are a few more of his favorites:

A cop pulls a guy over on an Irish street. The cop says, "Where have ya been and where are ya headin'?"

"Why, I've been ta the pub and I'm a headin' home," slurs the drunk.

"You've had a few drinks this evenin' have ya?"

"I did all right," the drunk says with a smile and a twinkle in his eye.

"Did ya know," the cop says, crossing his arms over his chest, "That a few intersections ago yer wife fell out of the car?"

"Oh thank God," said the drunk. "For a minute there I thought I'd gone deaf."

Brenda O'Malley is home making dinner when Tim Finnegan arrives at her door.

"Brenda, may I come in? I have somethin' to tell ya."

"Of course ya can come in, yer always welcome. But where's me husband?"

"That's what I'm here to tell ya," continued Finnegan. There was an accident down at the brewery . . . ."

"Oh God, please, don't tell me . . ."

"I'm afraid it's true. Brenda, yer Seamus is dead and gone. I'm sorry."

Finally, she looked up at Finnegan and said, "How did he die?"

"Aww, 'twas terrible, Brenda. He fell into a vat of Guinness stout and he drowned."

"Oh my dear Jesus. But you must tell me true. Did he at least go quickly?"

Finnegan shook his head. "Well, no, Brenda. Fact is he got out three times to pee."

Mary Clancy approaches Father O'Grady after a Sunday morning Mass. She's in tears. "Father, we need to talk."

He says, "What's bothering ya, Mary? Please tell me now."

She says, "Oh Father, I've got terrible news. Me Patrick passed away last night."

The priest says, "Oh, Mary, that is indeed terrible news. Tell me dear, did he have any last requests?"

"That he did, Father."

The priest says, "What did he ask Mary?"

"He said, would ya please put down the damn gun?"

A drunk staggers into a Catholic church, enters a confessional booth, sits down, and says nothing.

The priest on the other side coughs a few times to get his attention, but the drunk just sits there. Finally, the priest pounds three times on the wall. The drunk mumbles, "Ain't no use knockin.' There's no paper on this side either."

18

"You Have Gotta See This . . . ."

There was a nun at St. Mary's Academy who everyone called "Namu." I understand that this is really mean, but hey, we were high school kids in the late 1960's. Namu was a really big woman. The classrooms weren't that big back then, and they were all packed with about forty desks in each room. There were times when she would write something on the board, turn around to the class, and erase what she had written with her body. Naturally, her nun's habit (the long, black, dress-like thing they wore) would be covered with chalk dust every day. There was a story that one day it was pouring rain outside and Namu had bus duty. She put on one of those bright yellow rain slickers and went out to Reid Avenue where the busses picked the kids up. The story that was three first-graders tried to board her, thinking she was the bus.

Anyway, one day in class she gave us an assignment. We were supposed to be working on the assignment silently. Conor Flanary went up to her desk to ask her a question. As he was standing there, I saw him jerk his head up. I wondered what was up.

When he returned to his seat I whispered over, "What's up? Why did you jerk your head?"

"You have gotta see this," he said.

"What?" I asked.

"Just go up to Namu's desk and ask her a question," he said.

A few minutes later I went up to the front of the room and asked the nun a question. She was sitting at her desk and looked up at me. Then I saw it. She had one of the biggest boogers hanging from her left nostril that I had ever seen. She had a huge nose with huge nostrils, and this behemoth booger just about filled up her left nostril. It was about a half inch long. Part of it was green and part of it was a grayish color. It was incredible. I had to do everything I could to keep myself from reaching out and saying, "Here, Sister, let me get that for you," and flicking it off her nose.

To this day that was the biggest booger I have ever seen.

"Is That Nookie Green?"

One year after the annual Mackie MacGregor Golf Outing we were all sitting around, as Mackie says, "Drinking beer and telling lies." I can't remember who told this joke, but it gets told every year now, and is truly a classic.

A priest was hearing confessions one day when a guy said, "Bless me Father for I have sinned. I made love to a woman who wasn't my wife."

"And who is this woman, my son?"

"Her name is Nookie Green."

The priest absolved the man and began to wonder who this Nookie Green lady was.

The next man came into the confessional and said, "Bless me Father for I have sinned. I had sex with an unmarried woman."

"And who was this woman?" asked the priest.

"Her name is Nookie Green," said the man.

The next guy came in and said the same thing . . . he had had relations with Nookie Green. The priest just had to find out who this Nookie Green was.

That Sunday at church, a few minutes after Mass had started, into the church sashayed a tall, beautiful woman dressed all in green. She had on a sparkling green dress, a beautiful, plumed green hat, and shiny green shoes. The priest didn't recognize her, but he had to find out. As he was sitting near the altar he leaned over to the altar boy and said, "Say, is that Nookie Green?"

The little boy leaned over and looked at the woman carefully and said, "I don't think so Father. I think it's just a reflection off her shoes."

"Don't bitch at me . . ."

This joke was another one told while playing at Deer Ridge Golf Club. Good friend and fellow state tennis official Rich Hagen gave me this one.

A man reluctantly enters a husband-wife golf tournament at a local club. He is a fine golfer and a man with, obviously, lots of patience. His wife? Not so much of either.

On the very first hole the husband cracks a drive about 280 yards down the middle. The wife has to hit the next shot, and she dribbles a ball sideways into a deep woods. They use their entire five minutes to search for their ball and they finally find it. The husband looks at the green and sees he is totally blocked, but he has a chance to get it there if he can wrap a sharp fade around the trees. He hits his career shot and the balls rolls up on the green just above the hole, about three feet away. He's feeling pretty good. The wife then putts the ball way too hard past the hole, down the hill, and into the front sand trap. The husband musters all of his skill and holes the shot from the bunker.

On their way to the next tee the husband puts his arm around his wife and says, "Don't worry, honey, that was a bogey, but I think we can do better on the next hole."

She looks at him and says, "Don't bitch at me, only two of those five shots were mine."

Section III

. . . . Then College Was Freaking Hilarious

19

Grease The Oilers Night

Before I actually get to the story of Grease The Oilers, I need to explain a few things about college. I entered Defiance College in the fall of 1970. All of the movies you have seen about life in college are semi-accurate. For the most part, college in the 1970's was wilder than most movies can portray. One of the greatest movies of all time, "Animal House," actually came pretty close to capturing what college life was like in a fraternity during the '60's and '70's. I'm sure that many people who attended college in that era will disagree with me, but college life really was that crazy.

That being said, the very first fraternity party I ever attended as a pledge, was, in fact, a Toga Party. I know that "Animal House" made the Toga Party famous, but I went to one of those delightful events years and years before that movie was made. I took a sheet from my bed in the dorm and fashioned my own toga. I went out and broke off some branches from a tree and made myself a headband. The party was absolutely wild, but that's not what this chapter is actually about.

One day during my sophomore year at Defiance, Mackie MacGregor called me at the dorm and invited me to a party, dinner, and a wrestling match. Mackie was a pretty good friend of mine from high school, and he also attended Defiance College, but he really ran in a different circle of friends back then. We hardly ever saw each other on campus, but for this event he must have known I would have loved to party.

The party was supposed to start at 4:00 at McReynolds Hall, the dorm where Mackie lived. The theme for the Thursday evening party was "Grease The Oilers." Defiance College's arch-rival at the time was Findlay College (now The University of Findlay), and their nickname is The Oilers. For "Grease The Oilers" night we were all going to dress up in '50's and '60's clothes, grease our hair back, get pretty fired up (hey, we started partying at 4:00 for a 7:00 wrestling match!), and go en masse to the wrestling match.

Mackie and I had attended Lorain St. Mary's Academy and Lorain Catholic High School, neither of which sponsored a wrestling team, so we didn't realize how exciting and intense a wrestling match could be.

I went to Mackie's dorm at 4:00 with my hair greased back and my best '50's era clothing. We started drinking and partying. Basically, we were getting primed for an exciting wrestling meet. At around 5:30 we all went to the Student Union for dinner. When the party started there were only about ten of us, but by the time we went to dinner the group had grown to about thirty guys.

The two entrees that evening were fried chicken and spaghetti with meat sauce. Just about everybody got both entrees, and we took over one side of the cafeteria. We were all acting like savages, ripping the chicken apart with our hands and mouths, and basically being as obnoxious as we could be. Most of the other students actually thought it was pretty funny, since Defiance College is often a rather boring place, and our group of guys was definitely not boring.

Some time during the meal someone threw a chicken bone over his head and it hit someone about three tables over. A guy at that table picked up another chicken bone and fired it back. All of a sudden there were chicken bones and pieces of chicken flying all over the cafeteria. Someone yelled, "Food Fight!" and all hell broke loose. Things were still okay until someone did the unthinkable . . . he grabbed a handful of spaghetti and let it fly towards another table. Now everything was flying around. Chicken. Spaghetti. Jello, Chocolate milk. It got really crazy in a hurry.

We got out of the cafeteria as quickly as we could.

We all walked down to the gymnasium, a few hundred yards away. On the way to the gym we designed our plan for when we entered the arena. We walked in the gym in single file and in silence. There weren't many people there, but Findlay was warming up on the mat. We were all dressed up with our hair greased back, spaghetti stains on some of us, and we encircled the Findlay team. The leader of our group counted in silence with his fingers, and when he got to three we all screamed "Grease The Oilers!"

Once the match got started it was clear that it was going to be a very close one. Defiance College and Findlay College both had outstanding teams, and each individual match was very close and intense. Entering the heavyweight match Findlay led by a few points. We had to win the heavyweight match to win the whole thing.

That was not good news for us. Our heavyweight was a fraternity brother of mine, Bob Rote, and he was a fine wrestler. Unfortunately, Findlay's heavyweight was a national-caliber wrestler. In fact, he may have been the defending national champ. We all knew he was good. Our guy was 6-5, 265, and the Oilers' heavyweight was only about 6-0, 225. The Findlay wrestler was great on his feet, and he also was very tough if he got under your arms while standing. He had this great bear-hug move where he wrapped his arms under his opponents, flopped over, rolled on top, and frequently pinned his opponent. We knew that our guy had to stay away from the bear-hug.

The match was going along without much action when the Findlay guy got inside and got the bear-hug on our guy. We knew we were in trouble. Then one of the grossest things I've ever seen happened. The wrestlers' legs got tangled, and as they fell to the mat, you could hear bones breaking. Our guy had gotten some unusual leverage on the Findlay kid, and, as they were falling, the Findlay guy broke both bones in his lower leg. Snap! Snap! You could hear the bones break. The Findlay guy went down on his back, our guy stayed on top, and we won with a pin.

Everybody was going crazy and we rushed out onto the mat. Then I saw it. How grotesque! The Findlay wrestler's foot and bottom part of his leg was hanging there, attached to the rest of the leg by skin and skin only. I almost threw up. He was screaming in pain, and I certainly didn't blame him. That was disgusting to look at.

I don't recall if anyone ever got in trouble for the food fight. I was sort of lucky that no one really recognized me, since I was a Resident Assistant in one of the dorms at the time.

"He Chooses Death . . ."

Two guys on a safari are captured in the jungle. They are taken to the nearest village, where the chief of the village controls their fate. He tells the first guy, "You have a choice. You can choose death or you can choose Boonda. What do you choose?"

The guy thinks to himself and says, "Well, I don't want to die, so I choose Boonda."

The chief stands in front of the entire village, raises his hands and screams, "He chooses Boonda!" At that point every male in the village comes forward and violates the guy from behind. He is totally wasted, humbled, embarrassed. He may never be the same.

The chief tells the second guy, "You have two choices. You can choose death or you can choose Boonda. What do you choose?"

The guy looks at his buddy laying off to the side and thinks to himself, 'I don't want to end up like him.' He looks at the chief and says, "I choose death."

The chief steps out into the center of the village, raises his hands and yells, "He chooses death! By Boonda!"

20

A Very Hot Party

Another multi-sense incident occurred in September 1972. I was a member of the Tau Kappa Epsilon fraternity at Defiance College in Defiance, Ohio. Every semester the three fraternities on campus would hold "Rush Parties." We would invite a large number of young men to the fraternity house and have a huge party. The goal of the evening was for the active members to meet non-members of the fraternity and get to know them. Then, a few days later the active members of the fraternity would hold a meeting and discuss the guys who had come to the rush party. We would decide which guys we would invite to join our fraternity.

These parties were not at all unlike the parties from the movie "Animal House." There were always a few kegs of beer and other crazy things happening. It wasn't unusual for someone to rent a few porno movies and show them in someone's room, etc. They were generally wild affairs, and lots and lots of jokes were presented and remembered at these parties.

At the September Rush Party in 1972 I decided to liven things up even more. I had actually pulled this stunt the previous year, but the September '72 presentation topped just about anything I had ever done. I don't know where I got the idea, but some professional athlete had done it and I had read about it, so I decided to try it.

I lit myself on fire.

That's right! I lit myself on fire. Here's how I did it. I took a tight old pair of cotton sweatpants and soaked them in water. I did the same with a long-sleeved T-shirt. I wrung out the garments and removed virtually all of the water. They were just barely wet when I put them on. I then took an old, baggy pair of dress pants and an old, baggy shirt. I put those garments on over the sweats. My roommate then sprayed lighter fluid all over the pants and just a little bit of the shirt. He took out his lighter and Poof, I was on fire.

My next move was to walk down the steps of the fraternity house into the party. I walked around the party shaking hands and introducing myself. The flames crept up my body until my entire lower body was pretty much engulfed in flames. Now, the fire really wasn't supposed to burn much above my waist. (I also need to point out that my roommate had a blanket out in the front yard ready for me to roll around in to put out the fire) Unfortunately, either a bit of lighter fluid got high up on my shirt (would my roommate actually do that to me?!) or the shirt just burned faster than planned, but, at any rate, after a few minutes I could feel the flames creeping up my back close to my neck and hair.

Ten seconds later, as I was trying to get out of the house, I could smell my hair singe. By the time I got outside to the front lawn, I had lost some hair, I could feel the burn, and I could definitely smell the hair burning.

At that same fraternity rush party I learned one of the great jokes of all time. A fraternity brother of mine said the joke and everyone went crazy. I learned the joke the next day and have used it many times since. I tell people that it's one of the most difficult jokes in the world to tell because it is so hard to remember. About five years after I learned the joke and began telling it, a version of it appeared in Playboy magazine. The version I tell flows a bit better.

Two poets, Burns and Shakespeare, were up in heaven arguing about who was the greatest poet who ever lived. Both claimed the title. St. Peter finally got tired of the bickering and called the two poets together.

"Listen," St. Peter said. "I'm tired of this arguing. We'll settle this once and for all. Tomorrow you guys are both going to return to earth and write a poem. Whoever writes the best poem will be declared the greatest poet who ever lived. Sound all right to you?"

Shakespeare and Burns looked at each other, shrugged their shoulders and both agreed.

"One more thing," St. Peter said. "There's one stipulation. You have to use the word Timbuktu in your poem." Shakespeare and Burns both thought, "Wow, that's going to make things a bit more difficult."

They went to earth, came back the next day, and St. Peter called them together. "Let's hear these poems," he said.

Shakespeare said, "Mine goes like this . . . ."

> I traveled to a foreign land,
> I looked across the golden sand.
> A tiny ship came in to view,
> It's destination, Timbuktu."

St. Peter was pretty impressed. "That's really good," he said. "Burns, what have you got?" Burns said, "Mine's a little different. Mine goes like this . . . ."

> Tim and I into the woods we went.
> Saw three maidens in a tent.
> Since they were three and we were two,
> I bucked one and Tim bucked two."

Well, who do you think won the contest?

SL Defiance, Ohio 09-14-73

21

A Legitimate Expenditure

One day in 1973 I was walking through a department store in Defiance, Ohio with my college roommate and fraternity brother, Slick Kish. Slick was, at the time, the Treasurer of our fraternity. We wandered back to the sporting goods/toys section. It was a beautiful spring day and we were just looking to waste some time. At the exact same moment our eyes moved to a whiffleball set which included a huge plastic bat and a ball.

We looked at the toy, at each other, and before I could say anything Slick was rubbing his chin. He looked at me and said, "That looks like a legitimate fraternity expenditure." We purchased the whiffleball set (with fraternity funds) and returned to the fraternity house. It took us exactly two minutes to find ten guys who wanted to play home run derby in the front yard.

Our version of home run derby had us hitting from across College Place, the two-lane road that ran in front of the fraternity house. If you hit the house on the fly it counted as a base hit, but you had to hit it over the house for a homerun. If you hit the house on the fly but someone still caught the ball before it hit the ground it was an out.

The game became so popular that guys were playing at all hours of the day and night. There were times when we had ten or twelve guys on a team. That made it very difficult to get any hit except a homerun. Balls would be slammed up against the house and then caught on the way down for one out after another. The fraternity house, by the way, was a huge two-story duplex with two front porches. There were sloped roofs in a number of directions, so you had to be a wise fielder to catch a ball coming off a roof that sloped one way or another.

We played homerun derby for hours, and I'm sure that several fraternity brothers' grades suffered because we seemed to always be out in the front yard playing. If we weren't playing whiffleball, we were just sitting on the front porch "porching." That's what we called it, and we spent many, many hours porching. Of course we frequently had a tapped keg of beer as our friend sitting next to us. Porching also led to plenty of other mischievous adventures.

One day Bill Klein and I were sitting on the porch in the middle of the afternoon. One of our fraternity brothers, Matt Johnson, was walking across campus toward the fraternity house. It's important to understand that our fraternity house sat on the corner of Clinton Street and College Place in Defiance, Ohio. Clinton Street is the main street in Defiance, and it led straight over the hill to downtown Defiance. Even in 1973 it was the most-traveled road in the city of 16,000.

Anyway, Klein and I were sitting on the front porch and we saw Johnson walking across the campus from Defiance Hall. He was about a hundred yards away from us and Klein yelled, "Hey, MJ. Show us what you got!"

Johnson, in the middle of campus, stopped, put his books down, and took his clothes off. In those years streaking was a popular pastime, but not usually in the middle of the day so near the main street in Defiance. Johnson calmly took off all of his clothes except his shoes, reached down, picked up his books and clothes, and calmly walked the rest of the way to the fraternity house. He didn't run, he just strolled over to the house.

Klein and I, of course, were going crazy laughing.

Skilled Laborer

Another classic from the fraternity house front porch . . . . This was from a fraternity brother who could do voices and accents, which is just about needed with this story.

Sven and Ole worked together in a factory when they were both laid off. They decided to go to the Unemployment Office together. They each met with a counselor who asked them their occupation. Sven replied that he was a Panty Stitcher. When asked what that was he replied, "I sew da elastic onto da ladies cotton panties." The Unemployment Officer wrote "unskilled laborer" and decided to give Sven $300 per week.

She then met with Ole and asked him his occupation. He replied, "Diesel Fitter." She wrote on the application, "skilled laborer," and wrote out a check for his first $500 per week.

Sven met Ole outside the office, and, when Sven saw that Ole received $500 to his $300, he went crazy. He returned to the office and confronted the Unemployment Officer. She explained, "Panty Stitchers are unskilled labor and Diesel Fitters are skilled labor. There's a difference."

"Der's a difference, all right. I sew the da elastic on da panties. Ole puts dem over his head and says, 'Yah, dees 'ill fit 'er.'"

Farmer Brown's Pigs

Farmer Brown had twelve female pigs, and he wanted some more. He found out that the neighbor, Mr. Jones, had several male pigs and he hoped to mate them. He paid a visit to the neighbor and asked if that was possible. Mr. Jones agreed to allow his animals to mate with Farmer Brown's. Farmer Brown loaded his sows into the back of his pick-up truck and took them over to the Jones'. They were there all day.

When Farmer Brown went to pick up his sows he said to Farmer Jones, "I'm new at this. How will I know if it worked?"

Farmer Jones leaned against the barn and drawled, "Let me just say this. Look for unusual behavior."

The next morning Farmer Brown looked at his pigs and didn't notice anything unusual, so he loaded his sows back in the truck and took them back to Farmer Jones. He did the same thing the third day.

On the fourth day Farmer Brown sat down for breakfast while his wife was cooking. He told his wife, "Honey, Farmer Jones told me to look for unusual behavior in our sows, but I ain't seen nothing yet. You noticed anything unusual?"

His wife went to the back door and looked out. "I guess that depends on what you consider unusual. Right now there are eleven pigs in the back of the truck and one in the front honkin' the horn."

Another Farmer Brown Story

One day Farmer Brown's donkey fell into a well. The animal cried piteously for hours as the farmer tried to figure out what to do. Finally, he decided that the animal was old, had lived a full life, and was going to eventually be buried anyway. He went over and got Farmer Jones and they decided to just cover up the donkey in the well.

Both farmers grabbed shovels and started shoveling dirt into the well. The donkey realized what was happening and cried horribly. They kept shoveling and the donkey stopped crying. The farmers eventually looked down the well and watched as the donkey would shake off the shovels full of dirt and then step up on top of the dirt. The farmers kept shoveling and the donkey kept stepping up. Eventually, the animal was out of the well. He stepped up and trotted off to get some water.

The moral of the story: Life is going to shovel dirt on you, all kinds of dirt. The key to success is to shake off the dirt and step up. We can get out of the deepest well by stepping up and never giving up.

Oh bullshit! That's not the end of the story OR the real moral.

After getting his drink, the donkey came back and kicked the shit out of both farmers. The REAL moral: When you try to cover your ass it will always come back to kick the shit out of you.

22

"Did You Read Ralph Nader's Report . . . . ?"

I was a member of the Defiance College Speech Team for three years. The team was coached by Dr. Jan Younger, who, to this day, remains one of the most important people in my life. He was a mentor to both my wife and me, one of the three best teachers I ever had the opportunity to study under, and a strong influence on my teaching and coaching career.

My fraternity big brother, Jeff Rafsky, helped recruit me for the DC Speech Team, and, after a very non-descript sophomore season, I actually had a great time and lots of success in speech my junior and senior years.

At the end of my sophomore year Dr. Younger just believed it was time for me to break out and be successful at a tournament. He took Jeff and me to Gatlinburg, Tennessee for Pi Kappa Delta (National Speech Honorary) Regionals. The three of us had a great time. We have so many of the same interests, including sports, performance, etc.

One day after the tournament rounds we went out to dinner at a Lum's restaurant. I don't even know if Lum's still exists anywhere in the United States, but Lum's was famous for hotdogs. They had these beer-steamed dogs that were just wonderful, and you could order them about a hundred different ways. They had hot dogs combined with just about every kind of condiment, vegetable, sauce, etc, you could think of.

We all ordered two or three hot dogs with different sauces, etc. I was halfway through my first dog, as was Dr. Younger, when Jeff said, "Did you guys read Ralph Nader's report on what goes into these things?" Dr. Younger and I were both in mid-bite. We had both read the report. We stopped chewing immediately, and the attraction of our meal was completely lost. I don't recall spitting out the bite I had in my mouth, but I also don't remember eating any more of the dogs on my plate. What a way to ruin what, until that time, had been a delicious meal. Thanks, Jeff!

A post script to the story . . . . When I retired from public school teaching in 2005, Dr. Younger and his wife came to a retirement party thrown by my wife. He brought a very nice gift box. In the box were six souvenir Lum's coffee cups. Where he found the cups is anyone's guess, but it reminded me of the story about Ralph Nader's report in Gatlinburg.

Just in case you aren't familiar with Nader's report, the things that go in to hot dogs are definitely not things you or I or any normal human being would normally eat. Of course ground up, seasoned, and mixed with actual edible things makes the overall flavor of a hot dog more than tolerable. It's just that in Ralph Nader's report he made it seem, well, let's just say it stopped us from taking another bite.

An Easy $800

A woman was just getting out of the shower one morning. Her husband was ready and waiting to get in the shower. Neither had on a stitch of clothing. Suddenly, the doorbell rang. They argued for a few minutes about who would answer the door. The husband finally just stepped into the shower and turned the water on. Reluctantly, the wife wrapped a towel around herself and trudged down the stairs.

When she opened the door she saw her neighbor Jack standing there. He looked at her. "Wow," he said. "This is interesting. I'll tell you what. I'll give you $800 if you drop that towel."

She thought for a minute and then shrugged her shoulders and dropped the towel. He just stared for a few minutes and then gave her the $800. She felt pretty good about earning the money and went back upstairs.

"Who was at the door?" her husband asked.

"It was our neighbor Jack," she answered.

"Good," he said through the door. "Did he say anything about the $800 he owes me?"

23

The Real Story of *Blood, Sweat, and Tears*

It all started innocently enough when I was called to the fraternity house phone late one Thursday afternoon in February. On the line was a friend of mine who belonged to another fraternity. Thom said, "You ready to go? We'll be over to pick you up in two minutes."

I said, "Where am I going?"

He said, "BG. We've got a carload of guys going to BG tonight to party. We'll pick you up in two minutes." What could I say? By the way, the city of Bowling Green is about forty miles from Defiance. Bowling Green is the home of Bowling Green State University, one of the great party towns/schools in the country. There is no question that universities located in smaller towns are the best places to party. Just ask anyone who has ever visited Miami University in Oxford, Ohio or especially Ohio University in Athens. Bowling Green is in the same category, with great bars in the downtown (they call it uptown) just blocks away from campus.

I was in a bar called The Canterbury Inn, or CI for short. It was an upstairs/downstairs bar, and there was a band playing upstairs. I was separated from the other Defiance students when I noticed an interesting-looking girl. She was standing at a bar drinking a beer by herself. She was short with long, black hair. She had a sturdy build with large breasts and was wearing a tight white shirt and black jeans.

Ever the outgoing gentleman, I walked over to her and started a conversation. She was very nice and quite cute. Not ravishing, but quite cute. She was also very friendly.

One thing led to another, and we traded phone numbers before she said she had to leave. I think I put her phone number in my wallet, but, by the end of the night, I didn't really recall. I do remember leaving the bar with the guys I came with, and I remember calling "Shotgun" for the ride back to Defiance.

The next thing I remember was waking up with my face in the snow in front of my fraternity house. I had fallen asleep on the trip back to Defiance, and the other guys had pulled up to my fraternity house, opened the door, pushed me out, and driven away. The snow in my face sort of woke me up, and I went in and went to bed.

The next day I could hardly recall anything about the evening, but I did sort of remember meeting a girl. I tried to explain the situation to my roommate, Slick Kish, but he just thought I was bullshitting him. Unfortunately, I couldn't find her number. Fortunately, she found mine.

A few days later I was reading the local newspaper when one of the pledges called me to the phone. I picked up the receiver and said hello.

The voice on the other end of the line was barely recognizable. "Hi, Stephen?"

"Yeah, it's Stephen. Who's this?"

"This is Maria Magliori. I met you the other night in the CI. Remember?"

My first thought was, 'Who the hell is this?' "Uh, yeah, I remember," I lied.

"You have no idea who I am, do you?" she asked. "I had on the white shirt and the black jeans. You bought me a beer. Ringing any bells?"

"Yeah, sure, now I remember. Long dark hair, right?"

"That's right, long, dark hair. Anyway, as I said, my name is Maria Magliori. Maybe you've heard of my dad, Mick."

My mind started whirring. Mick Magliori. The name was familiar. I just couldn't figure out where. "I can't place the name Mick Magliori, but I know I've heard of it someplace. Where would I have heard your dad's name?"

She answered simply, "He's the Sports' Anchor on channel 13 in Toledo. You must have seen him if you ever watch the news. You do watch the news, don't you?"

"Mostly the sports, and now I do remember your dad. He's like a legend in Toledo, right?"

"I suppose some people would say that. Say, here's why I'm calling. My dorm is having a party this Friday night, and I was wondering if you'd like to come over."

I thought for a second and then said, "I think I'm okay for this Friday. Do you have any friends? Can I bring someone with me?"

"I think I can find a date for a friend. Do you know where Rogers Dorm is? The third floor is hosting the party and it'll cost you two bucks to get in. It's just a kegger, but it might be fun. Say around 8:00?"

"I will see you at Rogers Dorm, third floor, on Friday. I think I'll just bring one guy with me, but why don't you give me your number again so I can call you if more guys are coming or if something happens?"

That Friday night I went back to Bowling Green with Bill Klein. We found Rogers dorm and found the third floor. There had to be a hundred students in the third floor lounge. You couldn't even walk around. I finally spotted Maria near the TV. By the time

I fought my way across the room, I wasn't sure Bill would still be with me, but he got there, too.

Through the noise I said, "Maria, this is my good friend and fraternity brother, Bill Klein." She pointed to the girl next to her and said, "And this is my roommate, Amy Drexel." We all shook hands.

I wish I could say that the rest of the evening was eventful, but it really wasn't. The four of us left the party after about an hour and walked halfway uptown to a pizza shop where we shared a pizza. We all just sat there talking for quite a long time. When we walked back to campus Maria actually reached down and took my hand. How sweet. The kiss goodnight was okay, but nothing really special. I did notice that Maria had a good smell to her. I didn't notice it until we left the pizza shop, and I wondered whether the smell had come from there or perhaps the slight perspiration she had kicked up in the hot, crowded lounge party a few hours earlier. Needless to say, I didn't care where the smell came from, I just liked it.

Bill and I returned to campus and I wasn't sure if this relationship was going to go anywhere or not. I did travel to BG a few more times to see her, and she even came to Defiance to one of our all-campus parties, but it really wasn't too serious.

In the middle of March Maria called me up and asked, "What are you doing a week from Saturday? My sister goes to Ohio Wesleyan and *Blood, Sweat, and Tears* are performing there on April 1. She has tickets if you want to go."

Are you kidding me? *Blood, Sweat, and Tears* were great. They were one of the most popular bands of the late sixties-early seventies. I immediately told her that I would drive her down to Ohio Wesleyan, which is located in Delaware, Ohio, about two-and-a-half hours from Defiance.

I picked up Maria in BG on the night of the concert, and she looked nice. She was wearing a deep maroon peasants' blouse with tight jeans. Her hair was pulled back in a thick ponytail. All the way down to Ohio Wesleyan we were excited about the concert. It was one of the rare, hot spring days for Ohio. Usually it stays cold in Ohio until May, but every once in awhile a hot day jumps up in the early spring. You can always tell when that happens because college kids get out and start sunning themselves.

We got to Ohio Wesleyan and found Maria's sister's dorm. She and her boyfriend were waiting for us, anxious to get there. Even though there were supposed to be reserved seats, they explained to us that concerts in the old OWU field house were a bit disorganized, and that once the concert started everyone would be standing up on the floor in front of the band in one huge jumbled, mess.

As mentioned, it was a hot day, and it turned into an even hotter evening. The old field house was not air-conditioned, and it actually seemed like they were pumping hot air into the place. It had to be well over 100 degrees in that place. Everyone was sweating like mad, and perspiration soon seeped through Maria maroon blouse. It was very uncomfortable, but once the concert started no one seemed to notice. Everybody was going crazy, and the intense energy in the place raised the temperature another ten degrees. It was stifling.

Maria and her sister went to the restroom four times during the concert, which I thought was a bit unusual considering that we hadn't been drinking too much before we went. Except for the intense heat, everybody had a great time. We said goodbye to her sister and got back in my 1961 Buick Invicta convertible. Our clothes were soaked in sweat or I would have put down the top of the convertible. The hot day, however, had turned into a typical, chilly spring evening.

Maria leaned up against me as I was driving back to BG. When we approached her dorm it was well after 1:00 AM. "I'd like to invite you up, but it's against the rules to have guys in after midnight."

I parked in the large parking lot near her dorm and we started kissing. After a few minutes of kissing Maria started crying. "What's wrong?" I asked her.

"It's nothing," she said.

"Well it must be something. Otherwise, why are you crying like that?"

"It's nothing, really."

"C'mon, what is it?" I insisted.

"It's just . . . . It's just . . . . It's just that I want to make love to you so badly tonight, but I can't. I mean I really want to make love to you tonight but I can't."

"Why not?"

"I just can't," she said.

"Why not?"

"Just because. I can't."

"Why not?"

"You really don't want to know," she said as she started crying again.

"Yes, I do want to know," I insisted.

"Because . . . ."

"Because what?" I was beginning to get and sound upset.

"Because I just started my period and I'm a heavy bleeder."

Aaaaarrrrgggghhhhh!!!!! Information overload!!!!! She was telling me way, way more than I needed to know.

That night I learned the true meaning of Blood, Sweat, and Tears.

Knitting and Reading

I just heard this one at the 2007 state tennis tournament.

A policeman was patrolling at night in a well-known spot for "parking." He saw a car with its interior lights on, so he pulled up and got out. He approached the car and saw a young man behind the wheel reading a *Sports Illustrated* magazine. In the back seat he noticed a young lady knitting. He used his flashlight to knock on the window. The young man rolled down the window and said, "Yes, officer, what can I do for you?"

The policeman said, "What are you doing up here?"

The young man shrugged his shoulders and said, "Well, I'm reading my magazine."

The cop pointed to the back seat and asked, "And what is she doing?"

"Last I checked she was knitting a sweater for her dad."

The cop was totally confused. Here was a young couple alone in a car at night doing nothing but reading and knitting. The cop asked, "How old are you young man?"

"I'm 21, sir."

"And her, what's her age?"

The young man looked at his watch and said, "She'll be eighteen in about 20 minutes."

The Prescription

A woman walks into a pharmacy and says to the pharmacist, "I need some cyanide."

The pharmacist looks at her with some suspicion and asks, "Why do you need cyanide?"

The lady looks at him and says, "Because I want to poison and kill my husband."

The pharmacist looks responded, "I can't give you cyanide to kill your husband. That's against the law! They'll throw us both in jail and I'll lose my license!"

The lady calmly reaches into her purse and takes out a picture of her husband in bed with the pharmacist's wife. She hands it to him.

He looks at the picture and says, "Well now ma'm. You didn't tell me you had a prescription."

24

The 4-S-O

I honestly don't remember how it started, but The 4-S-O Golf Tournament certainly offered some of the funniest moments in my entire life. Let me explain.

My three best friends in college were Stevie Hopman, Steve (Slick) Kish, and Bill Klein. All three were fraternity brothers of mine and all three were in my wedding. All three were outstanding athletes and all three loved to party. I guess the simplest thing to do would be to credit Bill with creating the 4-S-O. There is a golf course just north of Defiance, Ohio named St. Stephen's. Until 1990 or so it was a plain, flat, nine-hole layout that was cheap and not very nice. In fact, it was one of the least nice courses any of us had ever, or have ever, played. The best thing about St. Stephen's is that back in the 70's and 80's hardly anyone ever played on the course, so we were able to play the 4-S-O there with little trouble.

In fact, in the fall of 1973 I was student teaching at Defiance High School. I came home from the school and Bill asked me if I wanted to get in a quick nine holes. It was a beautiful fall afternoon. We went to St. Stephen's, which is only a few miles north of Defiance, and entered the pro shop-bar-restaurant. It was all in one building. When we paid our $5 and signed in, we noticed that we were the first names on the play list for the day. It was around 4:00 in the afternoon and we were the first people to play the course that day! How could they stay in business?

By the way, are you getting the point of the name of the tournament? "The 4-S-O." Stephen Francis, Stevie (Hops) Hopman, Steve (Slick) Kish, and St. Stephen's Golf Course. Got it? Hey, Bill, the only one whose name is not in the title came up with the name of the outing. I don't think he wanted his name attached in any way, shape or form to this event.

Once we decided to make this an actual event, we had to come up with some rules. Most of the rules for this golf event were established before the very first tournament, and, despite a few minor tweaks here and there, remained in place throughout the thirteen years we played the event.

1. No colored golf balls allowed (like any of us would use a colored golf ball anyway!).
2. Only broken tees allowed.
3. Each player shall carry and use only two clubs plus a putter. Players shall use their own discretion in selecting which clubs to use.
4. Sharing of clubs is encouraged.
5. Furthest from the hole shall play first.
6. There shall be no marking of balls on the green. Sending and stymies are allowed and encouraged. OK, picture this if you will . . . my partner makes a long putt for a birdie. I am the next to play, and my opponent's ball is three feet from the hole. It is perfectly legal for me to putt my ball just in front of my opponent's birdie putt. I cannot mark my ball and give him a line to the hole. He can either go around my ball—probably using another stroke—or try to putt his ball **through** my ball. For that matter, if he is six inches from the hole for a matching birdie putt, I can putt up behind him and "send" his ball by striking it with mine. A sent ball must remain in play. If I send an opponent's ball he then has to play next—using the "furthest from the hole" rule. For that matter, if my partner has used three strokes and is very close to the hole, I can putt up behind him and use my ball to tap his ball into the hole for a score of three. Is this too confusing? Sometimes play on the green could take ten minutes or so, with all the strategy of sendings and stymies.
7. A player shall pick up after a triple bogey stroke. This means you couldn't hack around all day on the green. You only have seven strokes to do all that sending and stymie-ing on a par-four hole.
8. Players must have an open can of Goebel beer at all times. Two stroke penalty for violating this rule.
9. No golf shoes allowed.
10. The first hole shall be played in regulation from tee to green. The player/players who win the first hole shall "design" the second hole. Any team winning a hole gets to design the next hole. What does design mean? Well, after the first hole we would stand on the second tee and pick out which green we would play to next. We might, and often did, stand on the second tee and decide to play a par six to the number seven green all the way across the course. We might stand

on the second tee and play a very short par three right back to the number one green. The design for the next hole was totally at the discretion of the previous winners. We did have a rule encouraging discussion and suggestions for the design of each hole.

Are you beginning to see how this could be an incredibly entertaining day? We set the time of 12:37 as the official starting time each year, and we always played into the dark. In fact, we usually lined out cars up facing the ninth green of the course so we could go to our cars and turn the headlights on to finish the last hole. We always brought plenty of food and drink (especially drink!) It was usually very warm when we played, and with the "open beer at all time rule," we drank an awful lot of beer. We generally had four cases of beer on ice in big coolers in the car, and we always carried smaller coolers on pull-carts. In fact, that was another unwritten rule: the loser of the previous hole had to pull the cooler-cart until they won a hole. We also always had a boom box with music playing. Everyone had responsibilities for bringing certain things each year.

Even though the event was called the 4-S-O, we frequently had special guests. In fact, one year we had to have two groups of four. Whenever we had special guests we would usually just include them in our foursome, making it a fivesome or even a sixsome at times.

Three quick 4-S-O stories:

One year we were playing a hole from the 7th tee back to the 2nd green. In order to do this we had to cross the golf course, or at least cross holes number 3 and 4. It is very important to understand that we never played across a fairway in front of other golfers playing an actual hole. There were times when we had to play holes in the conventional order. We couldn't just hop around on the course in front of people or they would certainly complain. We were very careful about this, and in all the years we ever played the event, not one person ever complained. Ever. We were very careful.

So, we are playing from number 7 to number 2. All of a sudden there was a guy a little older than us, on a golf cart, in our midst. He asked us what hole we were playing. Remember, we are cutting across the course. One thing we never did when confronted was lie. We always told people exactly what we were doing. Then we offered them a beer. It usually worked, and it did this time. The guy joined us and played five holes, using our rules and laughing and drinking our beer. He was the club's greenskeeper and pro. When he told us who he was we were pretty concerned, but he was having too much fun to ask us to stop. I think he also realized that his course was not nice, we had paid to play, and we never trashed the course. We replaced divots, fixed ball marks, never left garbage around, etc. In fact, we thought we were improving that golf course. We were certainly making it more fun to play.

He had a great time playing with us for about forty minutes, and he even made some suggestions about possible holes. Needless to say, we accepted his suggestions and told him how great they were.

Another time we were playing from the number 6 tee to the number 8 green, making the hole a very short par three over the pond. When we all reached the green we noticed that a single player had emerged from the number 8 fairway. He hit onto the number 8 green from the correct direction as we were hitting from the wrong direction. Hey, that's the way the 4-S-O was played.

We all reached the green and then realized that his ball was also there. Oops. As he was approaching the green where we were standing, Bill Klein said, "Well, last year we played with the pro. This fucker is probably the owner."

The old guy reached the green and asked us what we were doing. Again, we told the truth and asked him if he wanted a beer and if he wanted to play a few holes with us. He accepted one beer and played a few holes with us. As we were heading down the wrong fairway on a hole he designed, he casually asked us what we thought of the course and the improvements that had been made. Our honest thought was, "What improvements?"

He explained how much nicer the course was this year and how the greenskeeper was doing such a great job. We told him that we knew the greenskeeper and that we had played with him the previous year. He kept asking us what we thought of the course. Bill Klein finally said to him, "Why do you care what we think about this course. What, are you the owner?"

He explained to us that, yes, he was, in fact the owner of St. Stephen's Golf Course. We had a really good laugh after that, especially when we recalled the Bill had said, "This fucker's probably the owner" just a few minutes before.

The end of the 4-S-O came just a few short years later. We were playing with just a threesome that year: Bill Klein, Slick Kish, and me. We actually had rented a gas golf cart to carry the cooler and boom box and sandwiches, etc. We had one cart for the three of us.

After playing a hole that ended at the number 2 green, we stood on the number 3 tee and aimed at the number 4 green. There was a large forest between these two areas, but about a twenty-foot-wide path had been cut through the woods. We could see the green we were hitting to, and it was about 160 yards through the woods. It was a very narrow chute, but a classic, traditional 4-S-O hole that we played every year.

We all hit our tee shots and then hopped onto the golf cart. We went right through the cleared out path through the woods. The area didn't really have a cart path, and the grass and weeds were about two feet high. It was somewhat dangerous driving through there, but we figured we could make it. Remember, all three of us got on the two-person cart. I was standing on the back bumper holding on to the seat in front of me.

About halfway through the area we noticed a high school kid cutting wood. He had a chainsaw and was cutting and stacking some of the trees that had been cut down years before to make the pathway. He looked at us and gave us a strange look. He actually said as we drove by, "What are you guys doing? We explained to him what we were doing quickly as we drove by.

After we got past him, I noticed that he got in a golf cart and drove away back towards the clubhouse. I remember thinking, "Uh-oh, that can't be good."

Within a minute we looked into the distance and saw a golf cart racing towards us. It had to be a super-charged cart. It looked like it was going 35 miles an hour. When it got to us we recognized the driver as the clubhouse manager. She was a big woman. She pretty much towered over any of us, and she was really mad. She ripped into us and called us just about every name in the book. Bill tried to calm her down, but she was out of control. She wouldn't listen to anything he said. She tried to kick us out right then, but we asked if we could at least finish our round. She agreed to let us do that (what choice did she have, we had already paid?).

After we had finished, I went back in to the clubhouse and tried to calmly talk to her. She had regained some of her emotions, but she just absolutely wouldn't even listen to anything I said. I explained that we had taken care of the course, had never, ever bothered anybody, and that we had actually played a few holes with the greenskeeper and the owner in the past few years. None of that made any difference to her. We simply could not play there anymore.

That was the end of the 4-S-O as we knew it, at least for several years.

I continued my friendship with Slick, Stevie, and Bill, and we still get together a few times a year to play golf, go to Cleveland Indians games, etc. The 4-S-O was actually resurrected for a few years ago by Bill Klein. The four of us got together, as we do every summer, to play a round of golf and then go to the Indians game. We tried to play at a public course in Solon, Ohio, Bill's hometown. However, it rained like hell that morning and they closed the course. What were we to do? After sitting around for an hour or so partying, I asked Bill if there wasn't some other course he could think of where we might get in a quick nine holes. He thought for a second and said, "I think I have just the place, and it's on the way to Cleveland. We ended up at a small, executive course called Walnut Grove.

Walnut Grove was not a very nice golf course. The pro shop was actually part of an old house. There were geese and ducks throughout the property (there were several ponds), which meant there was goose poop all over the place. The greens were tiny and the holes short. There were plenty of trees, and, as I mentioned, several ponds. This was perfect for the continuation/resurrection of the 4-S-O.

We arrived at Walnut Grove around 2:00 and instantly realized that we might have a new home for the 4-S-O. There was no one else on the entire golf course. The rain from the morning had stopped, but the humidity remained extremely high. It was one of those stifling days. 90 degrees with 90 percent humidity.

We rented a pullcart and started to play. It was Bill and me against Slick and Stevie, and all of the old rules were in effect. Stymies, Sendies, etc. once again ruled the day! We had our usual great time and drank a lot of beer. Remember that there was a rule that you must have an open can of beer with you at all times or there would be a two-stroke penalty. In other words, if you threw away your empty can before opening a new one, someone could call that penalty on you. I'm not sure that ever happened. You've heard about chain smoking? We were chain drinking.

We played Walnut Grove three times, and the last time we played it the young lady who took our money told us that it was their last day of operation. The Walnut Grove owners had sold the property to a real estate developer. The developer spent millions of dollars on infrastructure (roads, sewers, water lines, etc.) and hoped to develop $600,000 and up condos and houses. Two years after destroying a perfectly good golf course (that had continued a wonderful tradition!), guess how many lots the developer had sold?

None. Not a single one. If he had only known what he was ruining he probably wouldn't have destroyed Walnut Grove and we would still be playing there. Yeah, right.

Another quick 4-S-O story occurred in October, 2006. Bill Klein came through Defiance and we met at Slick Kish's house for drinks. It was a cold and blustery day, but I still encouraged them to go play some golf. Slick Kish called his brother, also a fraternity brother of ours and a veteran 4-S-O player, to join us at Kettenring Country Club, the nicest facility in Defiance, Ohio.

The four of us arrived at around 5:00 in the afternoon, and, as cold and windy as it was, there was no one on the course. We decided to play some holes on the back nine, since it was much more protected from the wind by the thousands of trees that line the fairways. It took us one hole to start having fun. We all had to carry our own bags (the clubhouse/pro shop was closed and the riding carts put away. Only crazy people would be out in this weather). We also had to each carry numerous cans of beer in our bags, since we re-instituted the "open can of beer at all times" rule.

Bill and I both parred the first hole, so we were one up, and no unique shots were even attempted. The next hole was a par 4 dogleg left over water. I reached the green in two, but I was about 30 feet from the pin. Slick Kish hit his drive into the water, so he was in trouble on the hole right from the start. His brother Mike was butchering the hole as well, but he did reach the green in three. My partner, Bill Klein, was about 40 feet beneath the hole in three, so he had to putt first. He drained the putt. He made a

40-footer! I putted next, and lagged to within about two feet. I was in perfect position. If Mike Kish got close, I would be able to send him or stymie him, since my partner was already in the hole.

Mike Kish drained the 28-footer. The hole was halved (tied) with pars and we were all laughing our asses off. We played about five more holes before it got dark, and every hole was loaded with laughter. We designed the next few holes, and, I swear, we improved the golf course. We played a 70-yard par three over trees, a 350 yard par 4 across a pond used for a different hole, and several other great holes. It's very difficult to understand how much fun we actually have with each other just laughing, drinking, playing golf, etc. I know we're grown men, but we all live by the same motto: You don't stop having fun because you grow old—You grow old because you stop having fun. I don't think we will ever grow old.

Finally, Bill Klein has been working for the same firm for years and years. He spent a number of years just in the office, and he finally decided that he needed to get out more. Thus, in the past few years he has traveled a little bit, and whenever he gets close to northwest Ohio he calls Slick Kish and me and we figure a way to get together, even if it's only for dinner.

At the beginning of May, 2007, Bill called and said that he would be in Detroit and, in order to return home near Cleveland he would be traveling through northwest Ohio. Being retired, I absolutely had to arrange to see him. Slick was originally set to meet us, but he had just returned from a Florida golf trip and couldn't get out of work again, so I met Bill in Toledo.

As I was driving north to Toledo, I listened to one of the local radio stations, and there were severe thunderstorm warnings. In fact, on my drive to Toledo I drove through a pretty severe storm. However, right behind that set of clouds I noticed a "window" of, what looked like, nice blue skies. I called Bill, who was on his way south to Toledo from Detroit and we changed plans, from just dinner to a bit of golf.

We met in Temperance, Michigan, which is three miles across the Michigan-Ohio state line, at a course called Giant Oak. We arrived at about 4:30 in the afternoon and couldn't believe how many cars were actually in the parking lot. Didn't these idiots hear the severe thunderstorm warning? They should be home or at work, not at a golf course where we wanted to play.

We rushed to the clubhouse and asked if we could get in a quick nine. The lady sort of made a face and told us that two leagues were ready to go off. They did, however, have an "Executive Course," and it was wide open. An executive course has mostly par 3's, with a few par 4's thrown in for good measure. Bill and I agreed to play the exec.

As the lady had said, the exec was wide open . . . in fact, we were the only golfers on the course. Our eyes lit up and we knew right then that we would be playing some, if not all, 4-S-O holes. We played the first nine in regulation and then decided to keep playing and play a few 4-S-O holes. Playing 4-S-O with two people isn't the same as having more in the group, but we played on. Once again, playing those crazy rules was so much fun we almost laughed ourselves to tears. When we finished and another storm was rolling in, we decided that we absolutely had to find a golf course that would allow us to continue to play the wonderful and unique 4-S-O.

Sometimes Telling The Truth Doesn't Work

I used to receive a daily golf joke from someone I never met. Some of them are actually quite good.

After an enjoyable eighteen holes of golf, a guy stopped in a bar for a quick beer. He struck up a conversation with a very hot redhead. After a few drinks she asked him if he'd like to take her home to her apartment. He was more than half drunk, so he agreed.

They got to the apartment and really had a great lovemaking session. His stamina wasn't great the first time, but an hour or so later he was much better.

On his way home his conscience started bothering him and he decided to go ahead and tell his wife about the encounter. He thought that she might understand that it was truly an unplanned encounter and wouldn't happen again.

"Honey," he said when he got home, "I have a confession to make. After I played golf today I stopped at the bar for a quick beer. I met a beautiful redhead and one thing led to another. I went to her apartment and made love for hours. I'm really sorry and I promise you it won't ever happen again. I hope you will forgive me."

His wife scowled at him and said, angrily, "Don't lie to me, you sonavabitch. You stayed and played thirty-six holes, didn't you?"

25

Road Trip! National Tournament Follies

Defiance College has always been outstanding in basketball. Perhaps the best team we ever had never made it to the NAIA National Tournament. In 1972 the Yellow Jackets ended the season 24-2, but the second loss was a real heart-breaker. The Jackets had defeated arch-rival Findlay twice in regular-season games, once in a holiday tournament, and once in the league tournament. That's four times we played them that year and four times we beat them that year.

In the NAIA District 22 Tournament we were set to play them a fifth time, with the winner going to Kansas City for Nationals. The gym was packed and we were really primed for the game. (That meant we started getting "ready" for the game around mid-afternoon.) The game started and the Jackets were playing great. The hated Findlay Oilers had no chance. Halfway through the first half DC led, 32-10. I will never forget the Findlay coach calling time out with the score 32-10. We were all making plans for Kansas City.

By the way, Findlay had a cheer they used when they played colleges that were located out in the country. The Oilers cheering section used to chant, "Go back, go back, go back to the woods. Your coach is a farmer and your team is no good." It was during that playoff game that I unleashed (with the help of the DC cheering section) our response. We had to wait for them to do the "Go back to the woods cheer," but when they did we unleashed the following . . . . Imagine a couple hundred fired up college kids chanting this, with jus the right pause at the right time . . . . "Go back, go back, go back to the city. Your coach is a jerk and your team is real _____." We just stopped. We left it up to the rest of the fans to fill in any word they wanted (that rhymed with 'city'). It was awesome. The entire gym loved it, even the Findlay people.

Findlay came back from the 32-10 deficit to beat us, 82-77.

The next year, 1973, we actually made it to Kansas City. I don't recall if classes were canceled at DC when we were out at Nationals, but it didn't really make any difference, we were all going to go. I traveled with Slick Kish, Bill Klein, and Sam Terrier, fraternity brothers and close friends. Bill had the nicest car, a 1970 Grand Prix, so that was the car in which we were going to travel. Needless to say, we had several coolers in the car for the trip. It is important to say that Bill decided that he would do all of the driving, since it was his car and he didn't think we were covered under his insurance. That was fine with us, since it meant we could party all we wanted, knowing he was going to be driving (and behaving!).

Defiance is about forty-five miles from Ft. Wayne, Indiana. We got in the car and I said, "Let's make a pact. Let's not start drinking until we get through Indiana." Everyone agreed. About five minutes later I said, "That's was pretty stupid. Let's make a pact that we don't drink until we get TO Indiana." Everyone agreed. Five minutes later I said, "That's stupid. Let's make a pact that we don't start drinking until we see a sign that says Indiana."

Two minutes later we saw a sign on Route 24 that said, "New Haven, Indiana 10 miles." Hey, we started partying! Bill, the driver, didn't, but that okay with us, since it meant more for us.

Hours later I was sitting in the back seat behind the passenger when I fell asleep on the way. My left leg was up on the middle console between the front seats. In the middle of a pretty nice nap I awoke with a start. My tennis shoe, a relatively new Adidas, was on fire! Sam Terrier had given me the old "hot foot." He had put three matches under the first lace of my shoe and then lit the matches. It burned right through the shoelace and started burning my shoe. It burned like hell and destroyed the shoe, and I was pissed for about thirty seconds, but I eventually wished I had thought of the idea and I got over it.

We arrived in Kansas City in the evening and went right to the Holiday Inn, where Bill had made a reservation for one room. We were all going to bunk together. He was standing at the front desk talking to the lady when the elevator door opened. I was right next to the elevator and I couldn't see the guy's head who was in the elevator. He had to duck to get out of the elevator. He came over and stood next to me. My jaw just dropped open. This was the tallest man I had ever seen. I came up to the middle of his chest. His head had to be sixteen inches long. Hell, his nose was six inches long, at least.

Understand that I had been partying for about ten hours, so when I saw this guy it damn near flipped me out. I started talking to him and found out he played for St. John's College in Minnesota and he was seven-feet six inches tall. In the state I was in he looked to be eight or nine feet tall.

We eventually discovered that we weren't registered at the Kansas City, Missouri Holiday Inn, but we were registered in the Kansas City, Kansas Holiday Inn, which was across the river from where we were. We drove across the river and checked in to our motel, which wasn't nearly as nice as the newer, larger Holiday Inn in Missouri.

As we were unloading our gear from the car, I looked up on one of the balconies and noticed a bunch of other college kids partying. I realized that we had come to the right place. Amazingly, when we went down the hall to the already-existing party, I ran in to two guys I had gone to high school with. Robbie Cavellini and Danny "The Rapper" Jackson were also there for the National Tournament. They were students and football players at Wartburg College in Waverly, Iowa, which was another school which had qualified for the tournament. We had a good time up in that room.

The Defiance College Yellow Jackets were scheduled to play their first game early in the evening of the next day, which meant we were going to have the entire day to get ready for the game. Slick Kish, Bill Klein and I decided to go sight-seeing in Kansas City. We particularly wanted to see Royals Stadium and Arrowhead Stadium, the homes of the Kansas City professional sports' teams. In case you aren't aware, those two stadiums actually share a parking lot, so you can see both of them during one trip. They were also very new in 1973.

We arrived at the stadiums and tried to get into Arrowhead Stadium first. It was locked up tighter than a drum. We couldn't even see inside the place, so we walked across the vast parking lot and tried to get in to Royals Stadium. We actually saw a small office door with the word "Security" over the door. I had on my Defiance College letterman's jacket and I went to the door. An old guard stepped out before I could knock and asked me if he could help me.

"We just want to see the stadium. We heard it was really nice," I said to the guard.

He looked at my purple-and-white coat and asked, "You here for the basketball tournament?" I nodded. "I'll tell you what," he said. "I'll let you guys go ahead and go in and walk around. We're pretty proud of this stadium. Just stay off the field." He opened a gate and let the three of us walk in.

We walked around the lower bowl of the stadium in awe. Royals Stadium is really nice. We then walked down to the bottom of the stadium. There was a small gate right next to one of the dugouts. The gate was open. Uh-oh. This looked like an invitation to us to go out on the field. The three of us just looked at each other and smiled. We were going out on that field.

We walked out on to the field and just looked around for a few minutes. The areas around the bases were covered with plastic tarps. There was no way we could resist. I stepped out onto the tarp near first base and acted like I was leading off. I was watching the pitcher (imaginary pitcher). I led off. I dove back to the base as if the pitcher tried to pick me off by throwing over to first. I led off again. This time I took off to try and steal second base. I sprinted towards second and did a head-first slide onto the tarp, stealing second base.

Slick and Bill were laughing their asses off. After stealing second I decided to go out and play the outfield. I went to center field and acted like I was really playing the game. Slick and Bill were sitting in the dugout. I yelled, "It's a long fly deep to center field. Back goes Francis . . . ." I backpedaled all the way to the wall. I jumped as high as I could, and, with my imaginary glove made a fabulous catch to rob the imaginary hitter of a home run. I then threw a strike to home plate, getting the imaginary runner on third who had tagged up. It was an incredible imaginary play!

Just then we heard the security guard's loud voice. "What the hell are you doing on that field? Get the hell off that field!" Oops. He came rushing down the steps of the stadium towards the dugout. He was pretty upset with us and walked us immediately out of the stadium. We had a hard time not chuckling as he led us out. I had made a spectacular play!

Defiance College lost the first game they played in the tournament.

Happy Halloween

The front porch or our fraternity house was one of the greatest sources for truly funny jokes. We would sit around for hours and hours just talking, telling stories and jokes, etc. The hours on the front porch were truly some of the best hours of my entire life.

A guy was in the hospital for a series of tests, and they had given him all sorts of medicine that really played havoc on his system. He got out of bed numerous times because he thought he had to take a crap, but each time proved to be a false alarm. An hour later he really thought he had to go, but he was tired of getting up and nothing coming out, so he decide to stay put in the bed. Oops, big mistake. He let loose with a turd-and-diarrhea-laced explosion that filled the bed.

He didn't now what to do and was very embarrassed. He gathered up the sheets and threw them out the window.

An old drunk happened to be walking past the hospital at that time. The entire pile of filthy sheets landed on him. He started yelling, cursing, and swinging his arms violently, trying to get the unknown pile off of him. Eventually, the sheets were in a pile at his feet. As the drunk stood there, unsteady on his feet and staring down at the sheets, a hospital security guard, barely unable to stop himself from laughing, walked over and asked what was going on.

The drunk, still staring down, shook his head and replied, "I'm not really sure, but I think I just beat the shit out of a ghost."

26

Snowball Stories

While I'm still talking about the fraternity porch, I have to tell a few of the best snowball stories. All through college (and high school for that matter) I always enjoyed throwing snowballs at moving vehicles. It just is fun to try and hit a moving vehicle with a well-formed snowball or iceball. It's also usually fun to see what happens after you hit a car or truck.

As mentioned, Clinton Street in Defiance is the main drag. At the front of Defiance College there are many large trees just off of Clinton Street. It's perfect snowball throwing territory. You can step out behind a tree, fire the snowball, and then step back behind the tree to become invisible. Stevie Hopman and I were the two big snowball throwers. We did it frequently and we did it well.

One night we were having our usual fun hitting cars and trucks as they went by. We always watched to see if a car would slow down or if we recognized a car we had already hit. We were throwing at just about every car that went by, and suddenly a large, blue Chevy stopped. We realized that we had hit this car before and that it had gone around the block to try and catch us.

Sometimes, if we had enough fraternity brothers with us, we would all simply step out from behind the trees and wave at the driver. What was he going to do, charge into the middle of ten or twelve college kids? This night, however, it was just Hopman and me, so when the guy got out of his car and started running towards us, we started running away from him. We had to run "into" campus. We were running together and we looked back and saw the guy still chasing us. We came to a place on campus where the sidewalks split and I yelled to Hopman, "Split up. You go that way and I'll go this way."

I looked back a second later and the guy was still chasing me. "Why me," I thought. "Why not Hopman?" I headed towards Sisson Hall, which was a very old building and had plenty of places to hide. I ran around the back of the building and down the steps into the basement. There was a sort-of Rec Room down there. It had a pop machine and a television mounted on the wall in the corner. The furniture was set up like a theater. There were two old couches with the legs removed in the front row. There were three old couches right behind those, and there were three or four other couches set up on cinder blocks for the back row. Fifteen or twenty guys could watch a football game in the room.

I knew where the light switch was, so I turned the lights off quickly and dove under the couches that were raised off the floor. The only light in the room came from the pop machine. I laid there under the couch for a few seconds when I heard the door open. I held my breath as I saw a pair of feet walk past me. Admittedly, I was scared. The guy chasing me didn't know where the light switch was, so he was sort-of stumbling around in the semi-darkness. Again I saw his feet go past me, not more than a foot or so away from my hiding place. Finally, after what seemed like a long, long time, he left. I stayed under the couch in the semi-darkness until a student who lived in the dorm came down the interior steps. He walked right over and turned the lights on, and I knew it wasn't the guy chasing me.

I rolled out from under the couch and he said, "What the hell?"

"I was throwing snowballs and I hit a guy's car," I explained. "He chased me into here. Could you do me a favor? Walk outside and see if there's a guy just standing around waiting."

The student came back thirty seconds later and said, "I don't think there's anybody out there. At least I didn't see anybody."

I waited another ten minutes or so before I headed across campus to the fraternity house. I was sitting in the house for ten or fifteen minutes when I heard the back door of the house slam open and then slam shut. Everybody got up to see what was going on, since the back door was hardly ever used.

It was Stevie Hopman, laying on the floor just inside the door, huffing and puffing. We all started laughing until he explained that he thought he had gotten away when the guy chased me. He said he was walking back to the house when he turned around and realized that the guy was now chasing him. It's important to understand that Hopman was on the Defiance College JV Basketball Team at the time, so he was in incredible shape. The guy chased him all around campus and even off campus. Hopman left campus and started running through backyards and alleys in the neighborhood around the college. In fact, an unfortunate accident became very fortunate for Hopman.

As he was running away from the guy through backyards, Hopman literally got 'clotheslined.' He ran, full-speed, into a backyard clothesline. The collision knocked him flat on his back and stunned him. He did happen to roll over after the fall under a set of bushes. The guy chasing him ran right by.

Hopman waited a few minutes and then sprinted back to the fraternity house and came in the back door. We all had a great laugh about the incident that night. But that's not all.

The next day I was in the house and a fraternity brother who lived in Defiance was there. He was a native of Defiance and didn't live in the house. We called guys like him "Townies." He said to me when he saw me that day, "Francis, were you and Hops throwing snowballs at cars last night?"

"Maybe," I said. "Why?"

"Did you hit a big, blue Impala?"

"Maybe. Why?"

"Do you know who owns that car?"

"Nope," I said.

He told me the guy's name.

"So? Who's that?" I asked.

"He's a cop in Defiance. He was off-duty, obviously." I began to get worried. "He also teaches karate at the place downtown. You're lucky he didn't catch up to you. He would have absolutely kicked the shit out of you."

Wouldn't you think that an incident like that would be the end of my snowball-throwing adventures? Well, it wasn't.

Probably the best snowball-throwing story occurred in March of 1974. Defiance had been hit with a great deal of snow that winter, so when March arrived there were still piles of snow on the edges of roads, sidewalks, etc. Even when the March temperature reached the 60's, there were still piles of snow, and wet snow at that point made great iceballs.

One day in the middle of the afternoon Bill Klein and I were standing in front of the fraternity house. Stevie Hopman was on the porch. We were throwing iceballs at cars. Pretty stupid, huh? Hops had to throw from the porch, because he had on shorts and a T-shirt with no shoes. Hey, we were idiot college kids, right? We weren't throwing at every car on Clinton Street, but we were hitting enough.

Bill and I were right out near the road when a car we had just hit roared up to the sidewalk. We were no more than ten feet away from the guy when he jumped out of the car and came around the car towards us. Neither of us had a snowball in our hands at the time, but we still thought we were totally busted. Hops saw the guy pull up and jump out, so he ran into the fraternity house.

Instead of stopping to talk to us, the guy who had jumped out of the car ran right between us after Hops. We just started laughing to ourselves and followed him into the house.

The guy was about thirty-five years old and he was really mad. He was totally out of control. I mean to tell you that this guy was going berserk. He was about 5-7 and weighed about 130 pounds, but he was seeing red. He was also dressed in a very attractive black suit, and we all noticed his haircut. He had this high, sort of 'pompadour' haircut, not unlike Elvis or Wayne Newton.

He was standing in the middle of the living room just yelling and screaming about college kids throwing snowballs. Bill and I were standing there almost laughing out loud because he was so out of control. Within a few minutes, the other person in his car also entered the fraternity house. This guy was also about 5-7, 130, and he also had this big haircut. The difference was, the second guy was about sixty-five years old—obviously the father of the first guy.

Now picture this: here are two guys, combined weight of about 260, yelling and screaming out of control at a group of college guys. Within a minute or two every brother in the house came to see what was going on. We now had them outnumbered about fifteen to two, but they were ready to take us all on. By the way, one fraternity brother was missing at this time. Hops was nowhere to be seen.

I finally decided to take charge of the situation. I tried to calm the two guys down, and finally got them to just talk. There big complaint was against Hops, because they were absolutely sure that he had thrown the snowball, since he was the only person to run when they pulled up in front of the house. I certainly wasn't going to argue with them about who had hit their car with a snowball, even though the chances were pretty slim that it was Hops, since he had been on the porch at the time.

"Okay, how about this," I finally asked. "What if I get the guy who hit your car to come and apologize?"

"I want to see the son of a bitch," said the younger man. "I want to look him in the eye and hear his apology."

I went upstairs to find Hops. I went in his room and he wasn't there. I had no idea where he was. As I was leaving his room to look further, I heard something. I walked over to the closet and opened the door. Hops was hiding in the closet behind the hanging clothes.

"Hops," I said. "All you have to do is come down and apologize to the guy about hitting his car with a snowball. It's no big deal."

Hops said, "It may be no big deal to you, but it's a big deal to me. That guy's scary. He could have a gun. There is no way I am going down there to face that guy. No fucking way. Besides that, I didn't even hit that guy's car. You did."

I could see that he was serious about not going downstairs. I had to decide what to do as I headed back down the stairs. I reached the landing and stopped. "Sir," I said. "The other guy isn't going to come down."

The guy exploded again. "What the hell you mean he's not coming down. I want to face that chicken shit who hit my car and then ran. Where is he?"

"I'm going to apologize for him. He doesn't think that his snowball hit your car anyway. He's convinced it was mine. I just want to say that I'm very sorry about the incident and I hope nothing was damaged." I would be kidding if I said that I wasn't nervous. I was sort of scared. The guy was, after all, borderline out of control.

He yelled at all of us again and then he and his father left the fraternity house. After he left we all had a good laugh about the incident.

The postscript to the story is this: The guys with the big hair who came into the fraternity house were father-son barbers. They were returning from the funeral of their other partner, and their nerves were a little frayed. Eventually, many of my fraternity brothers went to their shop for haircuts, but suffice it to say that neither Hops nor I ever did. Do you think I'm going to sit in front of that guy with a razor in his hand?

Another Great Lesson

Once upon a time there was a happy, hungry little fly buzzing around a barn. The fly came upon a big pile of cow manure. The fly couldn't believe his luck at discovering such a delicacy, and be began to eat and eat and eat. Finally, he just couldn't eat anymore. The fly cleaned himself with his tiny front legs, belched a few times and tried to fly away. He soon realized that he had eaten too much and his wings couldn't get him off the ground. What was he to do?

The fly noticed a pitchfork not far away and decided that if he could crawl up the pitchfork he would be able to leap of and then fly away. He carefully climbed to the top of the pitchfork and took a big leap, only to realize as he was falling that he still weighed way too much. Splat! He landed like a rock and died on the spot.

Moral of the story . . . .

Never fly off the handle when you know you're full of shit!

27

"Back To Punt For Defiance College . . ."

As a speech major and sports' nut at Defiance College, I was asked to be the football and basketball public address announcer for a couple of seasons. I also did the same job at Napoleon High School for years. I like to think that when I announced I added a little pizzazz without being the obnoxious home announcer you hear at some venues.

During my junior or senior year at Defiance College I was announcing the first home football game. In the middle of the first quarter the Yellow Jackets got stopped on a third down play and were forced to punt. I hadn't done any research as to the special teams, so I was very surprised to see that my old high school friend, Mackie MacGregor, was punting for DC. Mackie was the center on the team and was about 6-0, 240. For as long as I could remember he was always the long snapper on the punt team, but you usually see thinner athletes punt.

By the way, Mackie could kick the ball. He could also pass the ball. He used to call himself, depending on what activity he was attempting, "The Golden Arm," or "The Golden Toe." He actually is a great athlete who could do those things, but he was also the best long snapper, and coaches usually wanted him snapping the ball and not passing or kicking it.

So, I announce this: "Back to punt for Defiance College, number 75, Mackie MacGregor." I thought I clicked the microphone off, but I accidentally didn't. Right after announcing who was punting, I turned to the guy sitting next to me and said, laughingly, "You gotta be kidding me." Those words were amplified throughout the stadium just like any other announcement.

Mackie's family wasn't too happy with me (there were a bunch of them there that afternoon), but I think he forgot about it and forgave me. I think. I hope.

Barroom Football

This is another great joke heard at a fraternity rush party. This joke, however, was actually told by a freshman "rushee," that is a guy not yet in our fraternity. Needless to say, after this story, he not only became a fraternity brother but I think he went on to become the chapter president.

A tall, thin, gay guy walks into a bar and stands at the end of the bar and loudly asks, "Anybody in here wanna play football?"

A construction worker in a flannel shirt looks over at him and says, "Are you kiddin' me? I'll take you outside and kick the shit out of you if we play football."

The gay guy says in his sweet voice, "Oh, no. I don't want to go outside and play football and roll around in the mud and get all dirty. I wanna stay in here and play barroom football."

"How the hell do you play that?" the other guy asks.

"Well, first of all you take a beer. And you chug the beer. And if you chug the whole thing down, that's a touchdown. Yea, six points! And then you take your pants down and try to fart. If you can get a fart out in ten seconds that's the extra point worth one point. Wanna play? Wanna play? Wanna play?"

"Awright," the big guy says. "This is stupid. You go first."

The sweet-talker picks up a beer and chug, chug, chug, chug, chug. He finishes the beer in about ten seconds. "Yea! A touchdown! Six points! Six points! Six points!" He then proceeds to take his pants down and grunts and groans until a little, pipsqueak fart comes out. "Yea! An extra point! I'm ahead seven to nothing. Your turn."

The construction worker looks at the other guy and says, "This is really stupid." He takes his beer and in one huge swallow chugs it down.

"That's a touchdown," says the gay guy. "But I'm still ahead six to seven, six to seven."

The construction worker takes his pants down and tries to fart. The gay guy drops his pants quickly, jumps behind the construction worker and tries to mount him while yelling, "Block that kick! Block that kick! Block that kick!"

28

SMF Productions

One of the most fun times I had in high school was when our friend and leader Fran Dunning decided that we would make a movie. We filmed the movie in July, 1968, and it was a masterpiece called "No Such Word As Slave." It was a Roman gladiator epic filmed in Super 8 mm.

As a senior in college I decided that we needed to try to top that masterpiece, so SMF (Stephen Michael Francis) Productions were born.

The first movie we made was called "The Rapes of Wrath," and, despite the name, it was not a pornographic movie. It was a murder mystery about a stranger who entered a town and killed a few people. It had about twenty scenes and was shot on Super 8 mm film. The movie starred Bill Klein as the killer and Sam Terrier and Stevie Hopman as the detectives who track him down. It really did turn out well, and we actually had some stunts filmed. For example, we had Bill Klein dive out of a second floor window at the fraternity house and land on the ground twenty feet below. It just took a bit of editing and a few takes to get something like that right.

Many people who have seen all three movies think the first one was the best, but we still followed it up with two more. The second movie was called "West Side Glory" and was sort of a rip-off of the classic "West Side Story." Our version had competing gangs of bikers and jocks fighting over the affections of one girl. We filmed this classic in March, and it was pretty cold. The camera we were using was battery operated and kept running out of juice. That meant that when we filmed something at, say seven frames per second and it was supposed to be twelve frames per second, when the film was developed and run through a projector at twelve frames per second everything was incredibly fast. For example, the climactic scene had the bikers and the jocks meeting in the middle of the college football stadium for a huge rumble. The girl they were fighting about heard about the rumble and went to stop it. You can see her running from the end of the field, and she runs a hundred yards in about six seconds. It's really pretty funny, especially the fight scenes.

The third movie me made was called "The Hassler," and was a bit of a rip-off from the famous Paul Newman-Jackie Gleason classic "The Hustler." The backdrop is playing pool, but there are plenty of hoods fighting against the good guy who was just trying to win both the big pool event and the heart of the mob boss' girlfriend. Slick Kish and Bill Klein are the hoods who really do rough up the hero in the movie.

It's difficult to understand how much fun we had making these movies and it's even more difficult to appreciate how well they were made considering the antiquated equipment we had to use. If we had had the modern-day video cameras who knows what classics we might have been able to make?

Modern Math?

A teacher friend of mine told a story about a phone call she had gotten from a parent of a second grader. The mother had been listening to her son do his math homework and he said to himself, "Two plus five. That son of a bitch is seven. Six plus three. That son of a bitch is nine."

"What are you doing?" the mother had asked the boy.

"I'm doing my math homework just like the teacher taught us."

The mother quickly called my friend and angrily asked, "Is that how you are teaching these kids how to learn math? That two plus two the son of a bitch is four?"

My friend couldn't talk for a few minutes because she was laughing too hard. She finally composed herself and told the mother, "What I taught them was two plus two, the SUM OF WHICH is four."

Can't Solve The Problem

A 75-year-old man went to a doctor for a check up. The doctor told the man we wanted a sperm count. He handed the man a jar and said, "Take this jar home and bring back a sperm sample tomorrow."

The next day the old guy brought the jar back and it was as clean and empty as the day before.

The doctor asked what had happened.

"Well Doc, it's like this: first I tried with my right hand, but nothing. Then I tried with my left hand, but still nothing. I asked my wife for help. She tried with her right hand, then her left, and still nothing. She even tried with her mouth, first with her teeth in and then with her teeth out, and still nothing. We even called Arlene, the lady next door and she tried too, first with both hands and then an armpit and she even tried squeezin' it between her legs, but still nothing."

The doctor was shocked. "You even asked your neighbor for help?"

"Yep," the old man said. "No matter what we tried, we couldn't get the lid off that damn jar."

Section IV

Funny Doesn't Stop
When You Grow Up

29

"Anybody Seen Hops?"

Stevie "Hops" Hopman is originally from Parma, Ohio, a suburb of Cleveland. He came to Defiance College to play basketball and tennis. He made the basketball team his freshman year, which is no small task. I was a sophomore when he arrived on campus, he became my tennis doubles partner, a fraternity brother of mine, and one of my best friends.

We often get together to play golf or go to a Cleveland Indians game with Slick Kish and Bill Klein. We usually meet the last weekend of the season (the Indians are usually out of the pennant race by then and it's much easier to get tickets). A few years ago we arranged to meet the last Friday of the season for drinks, dinner, and the Indians game.

Slick, Bill and I met in Solon and had arranged to drive together to downtown Cleveland to meet Hops. We met at a bar-restaurant called The Winking Lizard. The place was packed with "Yuppies" types from downtown Cleveland for a Friday evening of entertainment. It didn't take us long to find Hops, and we had a quick beer. For that particular game we actually had great game tickets as well as tickets to Jacob's Field's Terrace Club, the exclusive restaurant that overhangs left field.

We all had our own tickets to both the game and to the Terrace Cub, just in case we got separated. The only way up to the Terrace Club is by elevator, and they check your tickets for the club and for the game before you can get in line to get on the elevator. Once we all reached the Terrace Club we searched for a table and finally found one in the front row. What an awesome sight. Our table was, seemingly, just feet from the left fielder. The entire club is glassed in and it's pretty fancy.

A waiter came over and took our drink order and reminded us that the seats we were presently sitting in were actually reserved starting at 6:50, or fifteen minutes before game time. We understood that, and at 6:45 we all got up and headed for the elevator to go down to our actual seats in the stadium. Hundreds of people were trying to get on one elevator, so we knew that we could, indeed, get separated.

Sure enough, none of the other guys were on the same elevator that I rode down, but, again, we all had our tickets and we all knew where our seats were going to be, which, in this case, was in the top row of the lower bowl right behind home plate. Great seats.

When I reached my seat Slick Kish and Bill Klein were already there, but there was no sign of Hops. Since he is from the Cleveland area and had been to Jacob's Field at least a hundred times before, we weren't worried about him, since we knew he could have been on a later elevator.

The game begins. No Hops. Third inning. No Hops. Fifth inning. No Hops. Now we started to get a little worried. Actually, we just sort of laughed and thought that he might have gone back to the bar to see some people he knew. He never showed up. His seat was empty the entire game. We really started laughing and thought that something really special must have kept him at the bar.

It was funny that night, but it wasn't funny at all when Bill called me the following Tuesday and told me what had happened. Hops decided to go out to his car and get his jacket. Remember that it was a Friday evening in late September. As he was jogging out to his car, which was several blocks away, he tripped on a raised piece of sidewalk and fell flat on his face. Boom. Straight down. He never got his hands up to protect his face, so he hit his face on the sidewalk full blast. There were hundreds of people heading to the stadium, and even though he was jogging in the opposite direction, some people actually stopped to see if he was all right.

One young guy leaned over and said to Hops, Dude, you all right? Do you need help?"

Hops rolled over and said, "No, man, I'm all right. Just let me rest here a minute and I'll be fine."

The young guy looked at Hops and said, "Dude, if you could see your face you wouldn't say that you're all right."

Hops had a broken nose, a severe concussion, and several lacerations and contusions on his face. He was already a mess, and he had only fallen moments before. The young guy called for an ambulance and Hops was taken to the hospital and kept overnight. I have seen pictures of his face, and he really looked terrible.

We laugh about it now, (hell, we laughed about it then!) but it was actually pretty serious. Now, every time we get together out wives remind us to try and not leave anyone behind when we go to a game.

"Somebody Else Musta Shot It"

Heard this one in the Napoleon High School Teachers' Lounge one afternoon.

An 80-year-old man went for his annual check-up. The doctor asks him how he's feeling.

"Hell, I never felt better," said the old man. "Matter of fact, I have a 20-year-old wife who I just got pregnant. What do you think about that?"

The doctor considered the question for a minute and finally says, "I have a friend who is an avid hunter. He never misses a season. One day he was in a bit of a hurry and he accidentally picked up his umbrella instead of his gun. He got out to the woods, saw a squirrel, raised the umbrella and said, 'Bang, bang' and the squirrel fell over dead. What do you think about that?"

The old man looked at him and said, "Well, I'd say that somebody else shot that squirrel."

The doctor replied, "My point exactly."

30

Teachers Say The Darnedest Things

I taught high school for thirty years and many humorous things occurred in those years. Two of the greatest, funniest incidents occurred in a three-year period, and both times female teachers were involved. Have you ever heard someone say something and wished you had said it? Trust me when I say that just about every teacher who ever stood in front of a class wishes he/she would have had the opportunity and the guts to say what these teachers did.

A veteran English teacher was working with a class and she made an assignment. One student just sat there and refused to even open his book. She looked at him and repeated the assignment. He just sat there. The student usually was a disruption in the classroom, but this day he just sat there. She started yelling at him and telling him to open his book and get busy.

"I ain't doin' that," said the student. He and the teacher got into a pretty good argument. He finally looked up at her and said, "You're just picking on me because I'm a Mexican."

"No," she said, "I'm picking on you because you're an asshole."

Now c'mon, don't you wish you could have said that?

The other incident is even better. A young math teacher made an assignment and a student just looked at her and said, "I ain't doin' this."

"Oh yes you are," she said. "Now open your book and get busy."

"I told you I ain't doin' this," he responded.

"Listen," she said getting louder and angrier. "You open that book and get busy." She obviously had had enough of his attitude over the past few months.

Under his breath, but loud enough for her and just about everyone else to hear, he said, "Aww fuck you."

In the great tradition of Al Pacino's Tony Montana in *Scarface,* she said, "Fuck me? No, no no. Fuck you." Oops. She immediately went to the office and reported herself to the Principal, and she got a letter put into her file, but she also became an immediate hero amongst just about all the teachers. Everybody wanted to say it, but she just had the guts and the opportunity.

Fine With Me

A man left work on a Friday and decided to go out with his buddies. A few hours turned into a few days, and he spent his entire paycheck, not arriving home until Sunday evening. He was confronted by his very angry wife who yelled at him for nearly two hours. He didn't apologize, but he just sat there and listened.

Finally, his wife said, "How would you like it if you didn't see me for two or three days?"

Tired of listening to her complaining, he replied, "That would be fine with me."

Monday went by and he didn't see his wife. Tuesday and Wednesday came and went with the same results. Thursday the swelling went down just enough where he could see her a little out of the corner of his left eye.

31

Through The Screen . . . .

Napoleon High School has been the source of many of the funniest things I ever heard, saw, etc. One of these events occurred in June, 1979. The faculty and staff at NHS almost always had great end-of-the-year parties that often morphed into semi-wild-lots-and-lots-of-alcohol-consumed gatherings. Sometimes we even remembered what happened the next day.

One of the great parties was held at the end of the school year in 1979. On the south side of Napoleon there was a large, old two-story duplex home that was rented every year by teachers. The landlords just handed the keys over to new teachers as they moved into town. That house was the site of many of the parties. By the way, can you really blame teachers for letting it all hang out at the end of a school year? Teachers have very stressful jobs, and when the school year ends, it's very easy to get caught up in a celebration. I've seen and heard teachers do things at those parties that I would never have believed they were capable of. Some of the nicest, quietest teachers become pretty serious party animals when they finally get the chance. Many of us party all the time, which makes our strange behavior not-so-strange, but it's the quiet ones who really surprise you.

That being said, the three guys involved in this incident were definitely not the quiet guys on the staff. Butch Morrison was the head football coach at Napoleon in 1979. He was pretty crazy back then, as were some of his assistants. Hilbert (Hip) Klotz was one of the assistants in 1979. Hip was a legend around northwest Ohio. He was about 6-1 and somewhere in the vicinity of 300 pounds when he coached at Napoleon. He was a very energetic and enthusiastic coach. Kids loved to play for him. Hip wore shorts to every game, regardless of the weather, and it can get pretty nasty in northwest Ohio late in October. He would lead the team out on to the field before every game, and as he led the players out on the field he would do a somersault about twenty yards out on to the field. The crowd and the players would go crazy when Hip did the tumble, and it became a tradition at all of the schools where Hip coached.

One of the other assistants that year was Knute Newman. He had been an offensive lineman in college, and he taught math at our school. It's somewhat funny that Knute Newman was a math teacher, because, in his own words, "I don't like story problems. I can't figure them out." Knute was not really the kind of person that might come to mind when you think of a math teacher.

OK, so now you know the guys involved. Everyone attends this huge party and pretty much gets wasted on a Thursday night. The next day was the Great Lakes League golf outing. Napoleon was a member of the GLL then, so our coaches and administrators were always invited to attend and play in the outing. Coach Morrison and Coach Klotz were going to be part of a foursome that included Knute Newman. When they went to pick him up in the morning of the outing he wouldn't answer the door at his apartment. Knute lived in a ground-floor apartment in Napoleon.

Morrison and Klotz rang the doorbell numerous times and then knocked. When Newman wouldn't answer the door, they wondered what the story was. Newman's car was in his parking space. Morrison and Klotz walked around to the back of the apartment. They looked in Newman's bedroom window, which was wide open. Only the screen was between them and Newman. Newman was in his bed, snoring away, sleeping off a pretty serious hangover. Morrison got ready to yell at Newman when Klotz noticed a hose nearby. Klotz grabbed Morrison by the shoulder and put one finger to his mouth, indicating to Morrison that he should remain quiet.

Klotz grabbed the hose which had a nozzle on the end, and turned the water on full blast. The nozzle was one of those with a handle like a gun, which meant there was pressure building up inside the hose. Klotz got the nozzle right up near the window and then opened it up full blast, drenching Newman in his bed. Klotz and Morrison then ducked down like little kids and hid under the window. They heard Newman wake up and say, "What the hell?" He just shook his head for a second and then rolled over. Klotz stood up and gave him another drenching. This time Newman jumped out of bed and started yelling at the two coaches.

Do I need to point out that they didn't win the tournament?

Too Much . . . . Too Much . . . .

In the 2004 Presidential Election, candidates George Bush and Al Gore could barely agree on anything. Even when they did agree on something they had vastly different opinions.

For example, both candidates agreed that the movie industry was a terrible influence on young people. The Republican candidate, George Bush, thought there was simply too much bloody, senseless, violence.

The Democratic candidate, Al Gore, thought there was too much sex and nudity in the movies.

In other words, Bush thought there was too much gore and Gore thought there was too much bush!

32

"Aye, Pass That Rum"

Throughout my life I have been involved in theater. I was in high school stage productions, college productions, and I even have been involved in quite a number of shows as an adult, both for the Maumee Valley Civic theater and the Fort Defiance Players. Many people may think this is "unprofessional," but I just love to have fun with these productions, as do MOST of the other people involved. There might be some exceptions.

A number of years ago the Maumee Valley Civic Theater staged a great production of the classic historical musical "*1776*." I played a Scottish immigrant as a member of the Continental Congress. I got this particular role because I didn't have to sing and I could do a Scottish accent.

Anyway, throughout the formation of our country the Continental Congress always had rum on hand to celebrate the successful passage of anything. If a vote was successful then numerous members of Congress would pass around a wineskin filled with rum and toast the success. All through rehearsals the actors would yell, "Aye, pass the rum," and we would pass around a wineskin full of water or iced tea. Not on opening night.

I came to the theater early and filled the wineskin with about three-quarters rum and about one-quarter cola. It actually tasted quite good (I thought it only fair that I tested out the mixture). In the middle of the first act the actor on my left, who happened to be a very famous theater director from the high school in Defiance, Ohio, called for the rum and I handed him the wineskin. He put it to his mouth and took a huge swig, not realizing what was in the mixture. He coughed a little, but, even more than that, I thought his eyes were going to come out of his head. I, of course, had to turn away so the audience wouldn't see me laughing.

As the rest of the actors took a swig of the mixture they too got quite a surprise.

In another production, *The Sound of Music,* there was a famous ballroom scene. The director of the Maumee Valley Civic Theater at the time, Ken Neuenschwander, always made an Alfred Hitchcock-like cameo appearance. During the ballroom scene he appeared carrying a silver tray. On the tray were a few appetizers along with about two dozen condoms. As he served the appetizers and people reached onto the tray, they were quite surprised.

In the wedding scene between Maria and Captain von Trapp, the Bishop acted like he was blessing the couple and others with holy water. I was backstage with a squirt gun making sure there actually was water being spread on the actors.

Works Every Time

Bubba and Jimmy Joe boys visited the city and they decided to have a nice lunch at a fancy restaurant. Halfway through lunch Bubba noticed that a woman at a nearby table was having trouble breathing. He got up and went to her table.

He grabbed the lady's face and pulled it close. "Kin ya swallow?" She shook her head. "Kin ya breathe?" Again she shook her head. He promptly spun her around, bent her over, pulled up her skirt, pulled down her panties, and licked all the way from her asshole up to the top of the crack. The woman was so startled that she immediately coughed up what was lodged in her throat. Bubba went back to his table and sat down.

Jimmy Joe was shocked. "Bubba, I ain't never seen nothing like that before in my life. That was amazin'."

"Yep," said Bubba. "That old hind lick maneuver works damn near every time."

33

"Hey Coach, where . . . . ?"

I was the head football coach at Napoleon (Ohio) High School for five years. I was the head freshman football coach for fourteen years, and the school finally showed enough confidence in me to give me the head coaching position. I was the head coach of the smallest school in a league that happened to absolutely go through the greatest period of football the league ever had. Rather than complain abut talent, etc., here are just a few stories about incidents that occurred while I was coaching football.

Karl Yunker worked as one of my assistants for about ten of the nineteen years I coached football. Karl is a great guy and a very hard-working coach. He coached the linemen and also called the defenses for me for most of our time together. I trust him a great deal.

Napoleon always opens the season with the biggest game. The Wildcats play their down-river rival the Defiance Bulldogs. The rivalry has been going on for over a hundred years, and it's always a tough, hard-fought game. The second game of the season is always versus the Wauseon Indians, another big rival of Napoleon. Defiance is about thirteen miles to the west of Napoleon, while Wauseon is a mere eight miles to the north. Because the Defiance game is so big, it is sometimes difficult to get kids mentally prepared to play Wauseon, even though it should be just about as big a game as Defiance.

The Wauseon High School football stadium hasn't always been as nice as it is now. The portable visitors' bleachers used to be brought in each year and set up right on the track which surrounds the football field. Thus, the bleachers were very close to the sidelines. Players and coaches alike could hear fans very well, and often times vice versa.

On of the years I was the head coach Wauseon was very good. They seemed to be running right at us and right over us. In the middle of the second quarter, as the Indians were moving toward their third touchdown without attempting a pass, someone from the stands yelled out, and it was very clear for all to hear, "Hey coach. Where the hell are your goddamn linebackers?"

I didn't turn around or respond publicly in any way. I simply strolled over to Coach Yunker and said, rather quietly," Hey Karl . . . . That's a really good question. Where the hell are our goddamn linebackers?"

A Union Joke?

People often ask me, out of the clear blue, to tell a joke. I usually make them at least, give me a topic. Well, if the topic is union workers, here's the joke. I heard it at another fraternity rush party in 1974.

A little nine-year-old boy (what the hell, we'll call him Johnny) came home from school one day. His mom said, "Johnny, you really like to build things, right?" Johnny nodded his head. His mom said, "They're building a house next door. Why don't you go over there and maybe you can learn something from the workers."

Johnny went over and came back about an hour later. His mommy asked, "Did you learn anything today?"

Johnny nodded his head, and, when she asked him what he had learned he told her. "Today we're gonna put up the goddamn window. Awww, shit, the cocksucker doesn't fit. Just shave a dick-hair off the side and the mother fucker will go right in." His mother was aghast.

"You get up to your room, young man. Wait until your father comes homes. You're really going to get it then."

A while later the dad came home and the mom explained what had happened. The dad called Johnny downstairs and asked him, "Did you go over and watch the workers today?" Johnny nodded. "And did you learn anything?"

Johnny nodded again and said, "Today we're gonna put up the goddamn window. Aww, shit, the cocksucker doesn't fit. Just shave a dick-hair off the side and the mother fucker will go right in."

His father exploded. "Young man, we will not tolerate language like that in this house. You're gonna get a whippin'. Now go outside and get me a switch."

Johnny looked at him with a strange look on his face and said, "Get a switch? Fuck you, that's the electrician's job!"

34

No Wonder There Was An Empty Seat

Another interesting incident involving Coach Yunker occurred at the annual Ohio State Football Clinic. Well over a thousand coaches attend this clinic each year, which was held at the time in St. John's Arena and French Field House on the campus at OSU. After the Friday clinic sessions there was a huge dinner in the field house. A famous Ohio rib restaurant was catering the dinner, and, as you might imagine, a couple thousand football coaches tried to hustle into line to pick up their dinners. We knew that the line was going to stretch well out the door into the parking lot, and we also knew that there was going to be plenty of food for everyone.

Karl and I decided to go across the street to a very famous bar in Columbus, The Varsity Club, for a few beers before dinner. Basically, we didn't want to stand in a line outside the field house for a half an hour when we could be in The Varsity Club drinking for a half an hour. Every once in awhile we stuck our head outside the door of the bar to check the length of the line going in for dinner. When the line was finally down to a reasonable length (three beers worth) we walked back across the street to the field house to pick up our dinner.

By this time there was no line, so we got our Styrofoam trays with the quarter chicken and slab of ribs and started looking for a seat. Wow, it was really crowded. I finally spotted two empty seats at one table. We walked over to the table and put our trays down. We sat down to eat and I nudged Karl. Karl's a serious eater, and he didn't want to look up from his slab of ribs, but he finally did. I used my head to indicate that he should look to his right. Karl was sitting right next to Ohio State Coach John Cooper. Both of us made faces like little kids next to Santa Claus.

It only took us a few minutes to realize why there were empty seats next to John Cooper.

Within a minute or so I said hi to the coach. He nodded at me. He didn't say anything, he just nodded. I tried to make small talk and said, "Hey Coach Cooper. Coach Yunker here and I spent last Friday night at the Bowling Green clinic. We had a great talk with one of your former assistants who's now the head coach at BG."

You will not believe what happened next. Coach John Cooper basically started yelling at me. "How am I supposed to keep guys around when they get offered better jobs? He got a head job at BG. Colletto got the Purdue job. Another guy got a job with the Cleveland Browns. How am I supposed to keep those guys around when they get offers like that? Huh? Can ya answer me that? Huh?"

I was merely making small talk and he went off on me. Obviously, he was very sensitive to the subject of his assistants leaving OSU for greener pastures. I found out later that there had been an article in the Columbus Dispatch about that very thing, and it was somewhat accusatory towards Coach Cooper.

That's not the end of the story. A guy across the table felt the tension and tried to relive it by asking, "Hey coach, what are you going to do with all those tailbacks this year?" At the time the Buckeyes had Keith Byars, Carlos Snow, and Butler Bynote'.

When the guy asked the question and Coach Cooper didn't answer, Karl jumped in with, and he absolutely said this as a tension-breaking joke, "My high school coach would have made one of them a guard."

John Cooper really lost it this time. "What are you talking about? Make one of them a guard. Do you know how big our guards are? This is Big Ten football. Make one of them a guard. What's wrong with you?"

Karl just looked at him as he stormed away. We've laughed about that story many times since then. There was always a feeling that Coach John Cooper never, let's say, endeared himself to the high school coaches in Ohio. Ohio High School football is very big and very proud, and it seemed that in his tenure many of the top Ohio kids ended up elsewhere, and it also seemed that he tried to recruit out of state an awful lot. It also seemed like those Ohio kids came back to beat Cooper-coached teams as members of opponents, especially the hated Michigan Wolverines.

It's All In The Spin

Two boys are playing football in a park in Michigan. One of the boys is attacked by a vicious, crazed rottweiler. Thinking quickly, the other boy grabs a stick, sticks it under the dog's collar, twists the stick, and breaks the dog's neck, thus saving his friend from the attack.

A newspaper reporter happens to be walking by witnesses the heroic act and rushes over to interview the boy. He tells the boy, "I'll title the story 'Wolverine Fan Saves Friend From Vicious Animal.'"

"But I'm not a Wolverine fan," says the little boy.

"Oh, sorry," says the reporter. I just assumed that everybody in Michigan was a Wolverines fan." The reporter starts scribbling again in his notebook and says, "How does this sound? 'Spartan Fan Rescues Friend From Horrific Attack.'"

"But I'm not a Spartan fan either," says the little boy.

'I thought that everyone in Michigan was either a Spartan fan or a Wolverine fan," says the reporter. "What team do you root for?"

"Actually," the little boy says, "I'm just visiting. I'm an Ohio State fan. The Buckeyes are the best."

The reporter smiles and starts a new sheet in his notebook and writes, 'Little Bastard From Ohio Murders Beloved Family Pet.'

35

He Almost Couldn't Tell It!

When I was the basketball coach at Napoleon High School, I always tried to attend clinics, etc. to improve my coaching. One of the funniest jokes I ever heard was told on the way back from the Ohio High School Basketball Coaches' Association Clinic in Columbus in 1998. I had been dropped off at the clinic by my wife, and I had arranged to catch a ride back to northwest Ohio with a couple of very prominent, successful high school coaches from the area.

On our way home after the clinic they asked me whether I had ever had a bologna sandwich from Waldo. I had no idea what they were talking about. We stopped in the very small town of Waldo, Ohio. There is a local bar/restaurant that bills itself, *Home of the World Famous Bologna Sandwich.* That was actually painted on the side fo the building for all to see.

We go in the place and it's really not very nice, but, even in the middle of the afternoon, there were quite a few people in the place, which told me that the food must have been pretty good. I asked the other coaches what I should have to eat and they looked at me like I was crazy. I HAD to have a bologna sandwich.

I went to the bar to order my sandwich, still pretty leery about the whole thing. I ordered the sandwich and the bartender asked if I wanted it on bread or bun and what else I wanted on it. I asked him if I should have it on bread or bun and he said, "Everyone has it on a bun, but it's up to you."

I said, "Okay, I'll have a bologna sandwich on a bun. What should I have on it?"

He told me that the only way to eat the sandwich was with pickles and onions and maybe a little mustard. "Okay, I'll have a bologna sandwich on a bun with pickles and onions and a little mustard." I usually try to get whatever the specialty of the house is when I go out to eat.

When the sandwich came I couldn't believe it. The bologna was between three-quarters of an inch and an inch thick. It was enough bologna for all three of the coaches to share. I had to be half a pound. It was also grilled, which I really liked. The onion was a full slice of a huge onion, cut at least a quarter inch thick. That's a lot of onion. The sliced pickles were also piled on. The damn thing weighed well over a pound. As soon as I bit into the sandwich I realized that the pickles were not dill pickles, they were sweet pickles. I don't usually like sweet pickles, but the combination of the pickles, the grilled bologna, and the onion was a unique taste sensation. I was very good, and I recommend anyone traveling through central Ohio be sure and stop in Waldo for a world famous bologna sandwich.

None of that has anything to do with the next joke, other than the fact that the joke was told as we were eating our sandwiches. One coach just started laughing out loud. I looked at him like he was crazy and asked him why he was laughing. He couldn't stop laughing. He finally told the rest of us that he just thought of a joke he had heard recently and that it was one of the funniest jokes he had ever heard. We finally convinced him to tell the damn joke, but he really struggled getting through it, and that made it even funnier than it really is, but it truly is funny. Here goes:

A guy is sitting at an airport bar. His clothes are all disheveled and his face looks like he had recently gotten the shit kicked out of him. He looks over and the guy sitting on the next barstool looks every bit as bad as he does. This guy, too, looks like he lost a tough fight. One guy says to the other, "What happened to you?"

The second guy shakes his head and says, "Aww, it was horrible. I got here to the airport and went to get my ticket. The girl at the ticket booth was a beautiful blonde with a huge chest. I looked at her and meant to say, 'I need a ticket to Pittsburgh.' What I actually said was, 'I need a picket to Tittsburgh.' She came around the counter and beat the shit out of me, all for accidentally saying the wrong thing. What happened to you?"

The first guy shook his head and said, "Something very similar happened to me. I was sitting at breakfast table this morning with my wife and I meant to say, 'Honey, please pass the cereal.' Instead I said, 'You've ruined my life you fucking bitch.'"

Three Men Died On Christmas Eve . . .

I heard this joke while sitting on the fraternity house porch in 1972.

Three men died on Christmas Eve and were met by Saint Peter at the gate of heaven. "In honor of this holy season," Saint Peter said, "You must each possess something that symbolizes Christmas in order to get into heaven."

The first man thought for awhile, fumbled through his pockets, and pulled out a lighter. He flicked it on. "This," he said, "Symbolizes the candles at Christmas." Saint Peter nodded and opened the gates.

The second man thought for a second and pulled out a set of keys. "These," he said, shaking the keys, "Represent the bells at Christmas." Saint Peter nodded and opened the gates.

The third guy was struggling. He finally reached into his pocket and pulled out a pair of lacy women's underpants. He held them up for Saint Peter to see.

Saint Peter looked at the man with a raised eyebrow and asked, "And just what do those symbolize?"

The man shrugged his shoulder and said, "They're Carol's."

Nods & Shakes

I was playing the second hole at one of my all-time favorite golf courses (Deer Ridge in Bellville, Ohio) when I heard this joke. It's pretty classic, and follows the preceding story pretty well.

A hillbilly farmer had a wife who nagged him all the time. Morning, noon, and night, she was always complaining to him or about him. Nag, nag, nag. The only time he could get away from her nagging was when he was in the field working with his old mule, so he made sure he worked very long hours.

One day he was out in the field working when his wife brought him lunch. He took the mule over near the only shade tree in the field, sat down, and started eating. His wife stood there pointing her finger and complaining about this, that, and the other. Again, nag, nag, nag.

All of a sudden the old mule backed up near the woman, lashed out with both feet, and kicked the woman in the back of the head, killing her right on the spot.

At the funeral several days later, the minister noticed something rather unusual. Every time a woman mourner would approach the man he would listen for a few moments and then nod his head in agreement. Whenever a man approached him, he would listen and then shake his head no. This went on and on for quite awhile.

After the funeral, the minister spoke to the old farmer and asked him why he nodded his head when talking with the women and shook his head when talking to the men. The old farmer said, "Well, when the women would come up and say something nice about my wife, ya know, how pretty she looked or what a nice dress she had on, I would nod in agreement."

"What about the men?" asked the preacher.

"They all wanted to know if the mule was for sale."

36

"Nice To Meet You . . ."

One of the nicest, funniest people I have ever met is a former Napoleon High School football coach who, I am afraid to say, has to remain nameless. He was also, by the way, a tremendous football and track coach. I had some great times with him when I was the freshmen football coach, and I will relate one of those here.

I was the boys' tennis coach at Napoleon High School for 32 years, and this coach, we'll call him Les for lack of a better name, was the track coach at the time. Northwest Ohio can have some brutal days in the spring, but you learn to run and play in all sorts of weather.

We were hosting Clay High School in a boys' tennis match one particularly nasty spring day. It was about 45 degrees with a terribly chilling wind of about 25 miles per hour. The match was well on it way when I asked the opposing coach if he needed to use the restroom and if he wanted a cup of hot chocolate. He said yes to both questions.

The other coach and I went into the building, and we went to the coaches' office to use the restroom. Now, this coach also happened to be the offensive coordinator for Clay High School's football team, a team Napoleon had defeated 19-0 the previous fall. When we got into the coaches' office, the door to the restroom/shower was slightly ajar, and someone was drying off after a hot shower. We had to wait a minute or so until the person in the shower left the restroom area to use the facilities. I yelled, "Who's in that shower?"

Coach Les yelled back out (even though we were only about ten feet apart). "I am, who wants to know?"

I said, "Hey coach, you know who the Clay tennis coach is?" Remember, the guy is standing next to me, but Coach Les can't see him, even though the door is open about ten inches.

Coach Les answers, "Who gives a shit who the Clay tennis coach is?"

I respond, "It's John Boles."

"Who the hell is John Boles?"

"He's also their offensive coordinator."

Coach Les is laughing now as he begins to open the door all the way and step out into the office area. "He sure didn't coordinate too much fuckin' offense last year did he?" At that point he is in the office area facing John Boles and me. I, of course, start laughing my ass off as I say, "Coach, allow me to introduce you to John Boles, Clay's offensive coordinator and boys' tennis coach."

Even funnier than that, Coach Les was just drying his balls when I introduced him and he immediately reached up and shook John Boles' hand. Now that was really funny, because the stunned Boles took his hand and shook it!

For years Coach Les accused me of setting him up, but I was simply in the coaches' office to use the restroom. We have laughed about this many times in the years since.

Another Coach Les story occurred when we attended the Ohio High School Football Championship games at Ohio Stadium in Columbus. The OHSAA held the championship games on the campus of Ohio State University just twice. Since then they have been held at Canton's Fawcett Stadium and Massillon's Paul Brown Stadium.

Through my connections with the media (I had worked for both newspapers and especially radio stations) I was able to get press credentials to sit in the press box during the championship games. This is very valuable, because it can get very cold sitting out at the end of April watching a high school football game, and especially cold if you really don't care who wins the game. In addition to that, there is free food in the press box!

I went to Columbus with several members of the Napoleon High School football coaching staff, and we had two press credentials. I took one coach up to the press box, got him seated, then went back down with both credentials (basically, a media pass), took another guy up, went back down, and brought the final guy up to the press box. Thus, we were all sitting in the warmth of the press box eating the free hotdogs, soup, etc.

The only way to get to the press box at Ohio Stadium is by elevator, since the press box sits high atop the gigantic structure. So it was back and forth and back and forth in the elevator. When I was taking Coach Les up in the elevator, there were five or six other people with us. One of them was an old friend of Coach Les' when he coached in southern Ohio.

Coach Les recognized his old friend right away and shook his hand. As he did, Coach Les said, "Ahh, that thing never grew back, huh?"

I had no idea what he was talking about until Coach Les introduced me to his friend. I shook hands with him and realized that the guy had no thumb! He had lost his thumb in an industrial accident, I think. I was so stunned and shocked that it didn't occur to me until minutes later how funny Coach Les' comment was about, "Ahh, that thing never grew back, huh?" To this day I just recall that question and I start to laugh.

Heartless Bastard #1

A Pastor, a doctor, and a lawyer met to play golf one day. The first few holes were pretty uneventful, but around hole number 4 the group caught up with the players in front of them. There were six people in the group, and the threesome had to wait and wait and wait. It seemed like there were two people lining up every shot in the group in front of them.

The lawyer finally said, "This is ridiculous. We've been waiting fifteen minutes to play this hole. I want to find the club pro and complain."

Just then the greenskeeper drove by. The players waved him over and asked what the problem was with the group ahead.

"There are four blind players in that group, and the other two guys help line them up for each shot," explained the greenskeeper.

The group stood in stunned silence for a few seconds.

The Pastor finally spoke. "That is so sad and yet so great. I'm going to say a special prayer for those guys."

The doctor said, "That a great idea. I happen to know some of the greatest ophthalmologists in the country. I'm going to call one of them and see if anything can be done to help these guys."

The lawyer just shook his head and said, "Why can't these guys play at night?"

TD 02-29-04

A Shocking E-Mail

A couple from Minneapolis decided to go to Florida for a long weekend to thaw out during one particularly brutal Minnesota winter. Because both had jobs, they had difficulty coordinating their travel schedules. It was decided that the husband would fly to Florida on Thursday, check in, rent the car, etc., and his wife would follow on Friday.

Upon arriving as planned, the husband checked in to the hotel. He decided to open his laptop computer and send a message to his wife. He accidentally left off one letter in her e-mail address and sent the message without realizing his mistake.

In Houston, a widow had just returned from her husband's funeral. He had been a minister for many years and had been 'called home to glory' by a devastating heart attack. The widow opened her e-mail expecting to see messages of condolences from neighbors, relatives, and friends. Upon reading the first message, however, she fainted and fell to the floor.

The widow's son heard the commotion, rushed into the room, found his mother on the floor, and saw the computer screen which read:

> To: My Loving Wife
> From: Your departed Husband
> Subject: I've arrived

I've just arrived and have been checked in. Everything has been prepared for your arrival tomorrow. Looking forward to seeing you and I hope your trip is as uneventful as mine. By the way, sure is hot down here!

37

State Inspector In The Building

On of my greatest practical jokes ever occurred in the summer of 1999. It was during the Henry County Fair, and it was a doozy. First of all, let's get something straight . . . . The Henry County Fair is, by far, the biggest social event in Henry County each and every year. The world pretty much stops in the entire county during "Fair Week."

I am a member of the local Elks Lodge, and for many years the Elks sponsored and manned a food stand at the fair. The Elks stand was in a great position, right at a corner near the grandstand. To get almost anywhere in the fair you had to go past the Elks stand. I worked at the Elks stand every year. We sold all sorts of great food, including things like hot German potato salad, sausage burgers, and home-baked pie among many others. The top seller each year, however, were the curly fries. We had huge bags of potatoes in the back of the food stand and we would wash and peel them and then run them through the grinder creating long, thin French fries. The person in charge of the fryer worked long, difficult hours, and that was usually his only job. It was difficult at times just keeping up, since the curly fries were one of the highlights of the fair.

The president of the Elks at the time was a guy named Tom Zgela. He runs a large construction business and is a very hard worker. He's also a pretty hard partier, but, most of all, "Z" is a large, loud, fun-loving guy. He's certainly not afraid to tell a joke or two and never afraid to spice up his language, no matter who is around. Some people might call him a big blowhard, but I really like him. He is one fun guy to be around!

So, I'm working a shift at the Elks food stand. I am also loud and obnoxious (at least that's what some people tell me). I always waited on the window, calling out the orders as they came in, gathering the food, collecting the money, etc. I just thought that we should all be having a good time. It didn't hurt that the Elks stand always had a cold keg of beer tapped back near the potato slicer.

The slicer that night was another hard-worker, Matt Gloor, who happened to be the chairman of the Elks stand that year. All he did was wash those potatoes and run them through the slicer, with the result being huge buckets of thinly-sliced curly potatoes. When I entered the stand that night I said hi to everybody and Matt said, as he always did, everybody be heads up tonight, I hear there's a state inspector here tonight. I usually said, "Oooooo, I'm really scared." Tom Zgela was the fryer that night, and he said something like "Bring on that asshole. Where is he?" I started thinking and scheming. Hmmmmmm . . . .

When I took a break from working about an hour later, I went over to the Holgate Boosters fair stand, which was pretty close to the Elks stand. I looked into the workers at the Holgate stand and saw a basketball coach that I knew. I called him to the window and asked him if he knew Tom Zgela. This coach, Ron Engel, is a great guy, very soft-spoken, but also a guy who might like to be part of a good practical joke.

"Are you sure you don't know Tom Zgela?" I asked him. "Does he know you?"

Ron Engel answered "Yes and No" to those questions. I explained to him that we always talk about the state inspector coming to check the fair stands for cleanliness, food preparation, etc. No one has ever seen a state inspector at a fair stand, and that's pretty fortunate, since I can't imagine any of the stands passing a very tough inspection. I explained the story and asked Ron Engel if he would act as the state inspector. I knew that Zgela would be a smart-ass with a state inspector, and I also knew that Zgela would shit his pants if a real inspector showed up and started making inspections. The fair stand, was, after all, one of the top moneymakers for the club each year. We needed the money to fund the charitable work the Elks complete each year.

Ron Engel agreed to be a fake state inspector. The plot was coming together. He even told me that he had the perfect prop to make himself seem even more believable. I returned to the Elks stand to complete my shift.

About twenty minutes later in walks Ron Engel. He had a clipboard with official-looking papers on it. He walked in and just started looking around, frequently looking down at his clipboard. Of course the first person he encountered was the fair stand chairman, Matt Gloor, who was near the back door playing with the potatoes.

After a minute or two Gloor asked, "Hi, who are you and how can I help you?"

Ron Engel just looked at him very seriously and said, "State inspector. I'm just going to look around." The place got very quiet, except for Zgela, who was still loud and obnoxious while frying the curly fries. The fake state inspector finally got up to the front of the stand, where Zgela was doing the fries. Engel just watched for a second.

Zgela finally said, with sarcasm dripping from his voice, "Yes? Who are you and what do you want?"

"State inspector," Engel said. He watched for another second or two and then said, "When was the last time that grease was changed?"

Zgela looked at him and said, with all the smart-ass attitude he could muster, "I don't know. What year is it?" He started roaring with laughter.

Engel never broke a smile. He was brilliant. He wrote something on the clipboard. He then said, "What's the current temperature of your oil?"

Zgela, once again being a smart-ass, said, "How the hell am I supposed to know that?"

Engel said, "You mean you're frying potatoes in oil and you don't even know if the temperature is conducive?"

Zgela said, with a little shake of his head, "Well, I guess I am." He again roared with laughter.

Engel once again never cracked a smile. "You think this is pretty funny, don't you? I can close this place down in about a minute and a half, wiseguy. Now what's the temperature of your oil?"

Zgela suddenly got very serious. He was nervous all of a sudden. I was about five feet away, around a corner, and I was biting through my lower lip to keep from laughing. This was awesome.

Zgela got down on his hands and knees and began to search under the fryer for a thermostat. He looked and decided that the oil was, I think, 180 degrees. Anyway, he was absolutely a meek little lamb at this point. After all, the state inspector was on the premises, and he continued to inspect the place and ask questions. He asked Zgela a number of other questions, and those that Zgela couldn't answer Engel jotted something down on the clipboard.

Engel finally decided to leave, but told Zgela that he better clean the place up by the next day or he would be coming in to shut us down. I was really having a tough time controlling myself, but I managed to be just serious enough. Engel left the building, went to the outside, walked to one of our open serving windows and looked in at Zgela and said, "Hey, can I have some of those fries?" Engel smiled and just looked at Zgela. Zgela looked at him and said, "What? Who are you?"

Engel looked at him and said, "I'm Ron Engel. I work over at the Holgate stand." Everybody in our entire place started going crazy laughing at Zgela. He thought for about five seconds and roared, "Francis! You son of a bitch! I am goin' kick your ass. I owe you one, and you'll get it someday. Paybacks are hell you son of a bitch"

I was getting ready to run away from him, but I was laughing too hard.

Wal-Mart Greeter

I believe I heard this joke while sitting in the rain at Red Hawk Golf Course outside of Findlay, Ohio. We were waiting to play this gorgeous course.

A guy goes to Wal-Mart and asks to see the manager. The manager sees the guy and the guy says, "I want to be a Wal-Mart greeter."

The manager looks at him and says, "You're pretty young for that job, but I think we have something in Lawn and Garden."

"No, no, no," the guy says, "I need to be a greeter. You see, I have a unique gift. I can tell what every person who enters the store is shopping for, and I have every aisle memorized, so when they come in I just greet them and tell them where to go."

The manager can't believe this and says, "This I gotta see."

The new guy and the manager go to the front door. In walks a man and the guy says, "Welcome to Wal-Mart. The motor oil is on aisle 26."

The shopper looks at him and says, "That's amazing. How did you know that's what I wanted?"

The new guy points to his head and says, "It's a gift."

The manager is impressed, but thinks it could have been dumb luck.

A lady enters the store and the new guy says, "Welcome to Wal-Mart. The instant coffee is on aisle 11."

The lady smiles and says, "Wow, that's impressive. That's exactly what I came here for."

The manager is getting more impressed by the minute, but decides he wants to witness one more. Another lady, this one about six-feet tall, enters the store.

"Welcome to Wal-Mart. Feminine hygiene products are on aisle 6."

"What makes you think I'm here for feminine hygiene products? I actually came in for some toilet paper." She storms off into the store.

The manager shakes his head and says, "I knew that was too good to be true. I can't hire you."

The new guy says, "Hey boss, gimme a break." He holds his fingers about an inch apart. "I was this close!"

38

The Devastator

One of the greatest, nicest people I have ever known is a Guidance Counselor at Napoleon High School, Gregg Merrill. Gregg will do anything to help anyone. He is also one outstanding athlete. He was one of those three-sport athletes in high school, and he actually played two sports for four years in college, excelling in baseball and basketball at Youngstown State University.

I got him interested in tennis in one of my first years at Napoleon, and he naturally became an excellent player. He and I even traveled and played some 35 & Over tournaments, and he was very successful. Once he stopped playing tennis he then turned his attention to golf and has become an excellent golfer. He is actually the boys' golf coach at Napoleon High School.

Every spring for a number of years Gregg would organize a golf trip right after school ended for the year. It was pretty much a huge party for teachers and friends who left Napoleon, played golf, spent the night at Gregg's cottage at Devil's Lake in Michigan, played some more golf, played some poker, and, in general, drank a lot of beer.

I was an active player in these golf outings right from the start of them, and I really enjoyed myself every year. I am not a good golfer, but I certainly talk a good game, (present handicap moves from a 14 to a 16 and back) and I really like to have a good time.

One year we were going to start the trip at Ironwood Golf Club in Wauseon, Ohio. I had recently purchased a new driver. I actually bought the club at a Sam's Club Wholesale Warehouse for $29.99. I was telling everybody going on the trip that they would certainly want to partner with me, since I had the new club, named The Devastator. That name wasn't invented by me, it was actually the name of the club, engraved on the bottom. For a week prior to the outing I was talking up a storm about how I was going to be kicking some butt with The Devastator.

There were three foursome set to play that day, and I frequently walk up to the tee and play first. I must admit that I am a somewhat impatient golfer—I really like to play fast. So there I was, on the first tee at Ironwood Golf Club in front of eleven other guys, mostly Napoleon teachers. As you can imagine, there's lots of pressure for that first shot. There usually is also plenty of trash talking, at least before a player addresses the ball.

The crowd got quiet as I prepared to hit the ball. They had all heard the stories about how The Devastator was going to raise my level of play. I was ready. I took a mighty swing, and my follow-through, as it often does, was on too short of an arc. My hands didn't get away from my body, and the club wrapped around my shoulder instead of my head. In other words, my follow-through hit my shoulder. There was a strange, cracking sound. It snapped The Devastator. The handle of the club was still connected to the shaft and head by one thin piece of graphite. There I was, holding this club in my hand in basically two pieces.

It was only a second before the rest of the guys realized what had happened. It seemed that everyone watched the ball leave the club (it sliced at about 180 yards out), heard the sound, then looked back. When they finally realized that I had snapped the club, they lost it. There were actually guys on the ground laughing. Naturally, it was one of the great stories of the trip. They renamed The Devastator, giving it every crazy name they could think of. The Intimidator, The Ejaculator, The Constipator, The Fornicator, The Dictator, The Emancipator, I think I heard them all for the next few days. I guess I probably deserved it after all the big talk about how The Devastator was going to be so awesome.

"Ya Got A Problem With Yer Loft"

Three friends of mine were playing golf at an exclusive club near Cleveland one day. The threesome was just getting ready to tee off on the first hole when the starter came out to the tee and asked them if they minded being joined by a single golfer. Golf is a very social game, so my friends agreed to let the single join them. They asked the starter who the fourth guy was.

"He's a visiting pro from Scotland. Nice fellow. You guys will like him," said the club worker.

"God, playing with a pro. Maybe we'll be able to learn something," my friend said. None of the three were very accomplished golfers.

The Scotsman joined the others and there were handshakes and greetings all around. My first friend stood on the tee and addressed the ball. He promptly sliced it into the woods. He turned around and said to the pro who had joined them, "Any idea what my problem is?"

The pro looked at him and said, with a very distinguished Scottish brogue, "Ya got a problem with yer loft." Not wanting to sound stupid, my friend just nodded.

The second guy in the group hit a vicious hook into a nearby pond. He looked back and asked, "Any idea what my problem is?"

Again, the Scotsman said, "Ya got a problem with yer loft." The second guy nodded grudgingly.

The third guy addressed the ball, wanting to make sure that he hit a good shot. He topped the ball and it went about forty yards, not even reaching the Womens' Tee. He turned around and before he could say anything, the Scottish pro said, "You also. Ya got a problem with yer loft."

"Wait a minute," the third guy said. "He hit a slice and you said he's got a problem with his loft. He hit a hook and you said he's got a problem with his loft. I top mine and you say I've got a problem with my loft. What's up?"

The Scotsman was walking towards the tee and he said, "Ya all got a problem with yer loft. Loft. L-O-F-T. Lack Of Fuckin' Talent."

I think he had my friends tabbed pretty well.

39

Different Coaching Techniques

I coached football at Napoleon High School for nineteen years, including five years as the head varsity coach. I also coached tennis at the same time, and I have been accused of coaching tennis with the same intensity as I coached football. The two sports are vastly different, but I don't think that tennis players should have any less intensity than football players.

Every once in awhile (my former players would say it happened all the time) I would really raise my voice when correcting or coaching a tennis player. I rarely used any profane language, even when I coached football, but there is a time and a place for everything. I'm sure there are parents and administrators who would say there is never a time for any bad language, but those people either never played or never coached anything.

Another thing I did coaching tennis was really work on strategy with players. We might practice a certain doubles' move, after which I expected the players to execute the move in the next match. In fact, we frequently would practice a specific shot or move just before the other team arrived for a match. I tried to never expect a player to hit a shot we hadn't practiced, but I certainly did expect players to execute shots if we HAD practiced them.

Just about the nastiest I ever got coaching tennis occurred during a close match a number of years ago. Before the other team arrived to play the match we had practiced one specific move and shot. During the match my players weren't executing the move we had practiced. I called them over as they changed ends on the odd game (that's the only time we are allowed to talk to players). I got them very close to the fence and I said, through gritted teeth and with much intensity, "Listen. You guys get your heads out of your asses and start playing. We just practiced that before they got here. Start executing." I said it very quietly, but the players absolutely knew how upset I was. They responded and started playing better.

Well, when I stopped coaching football I began to coach girls' tennis in the fall. Guess what? There's a little more pressure coaching varsity football than there is coaching girls' tennis, especially at a school like Napoleon that, I believe, had never had a winning season in girls' tennis. I brought the same intensity, and I'm not sure the girls' knew what to do.

I just hate to lose, and I don't think there's ever a reason to just accept losing. So, in my first season coaching girls' tennis we practiced a certain shot and move before a team arrived to play the match. The second doubles' team that year was a couple of great kids. Both were blondes, one being a sophomore and the other a freshman. Both girls were quiet, well-behaved, intelligent kids. They really tried to do what I asked them to do.

The match starts and they weren't executing what we had practiced. I couldn't help myself—I had to call them back to the fence and talk to them. They stepped very close to the fence, just as the guys had. Again, I talked quietly but through clenched teeth and with great intensity. "Now listen." Both girls' eyes were very wide. They had not seen me like this before. "We just practiced that before they got here. Now get your heads . . . ." I stopped in mid-sentence as both girls dropped their heads and began to cry. I completely changed my tone and said, "Get your heads up." I was even more positive with the second time I said it. "C'mon. Get your heads up. Things are going to be okay. Let's stop crying and perk back up. Things are going to be fine."

The difference between coaching boys and girls is, sometimes, vast.

Another example of the difference between coaching boys and girls occurred in the school van as we headed to Port Clinton, Ohio for a tournament. It wasn't my first year coaching girls, but it was the first time we went to Port Clinton. I had been there dozens of times with the boys' team, so I knew the site pretty well.

We were sitting in the van and I said, "Girls, heads up. Listen now. I've been to Port Clinton before. The set-up of their courts is like this. There's . . . ."

I looked in the rear-view mirror and one girl was looking at the other. I heard her say, quietly, "Did you get your hair cut? It really looks nice." I was trying to coach these girls and they were talking about each other's hair.

"I Learned Wednesday"

One day at Tierra del Sol Country Club in The Villages, Florida, I was on the practice putting green getting ready to play a round. There were two women standing nearby.

The club pro came out of the pro shop and walked over to the women and said, "Are you two ladies here to learn how to play golf?"

The lady in pink pointed to the other lady and said, "She is. I learned Wednesday."

40

Open Mouth and Insert Foot

Every once in awhile during my life I have said something that was either terribly inappropriate or just the wrong thing to say at the wrong time. I guess being an outspoken person has its hazards, huh?

Teachers, like most other people, hate meetings. Teachers REALLY hate meetings. Most teachers' meetings occur after school, and the last thing a teacher wants to do, after spending seven hours with kids, is to sit and listen to an administrator drone on about, well, just about anything. I dislike teachers' meetings so much that I did just about anything I could to skip them, up-to-and-including scheduling dentist appointments on days when I knew we were schedule to meet. When I did go to teachers' meetings, all the other teachers knew I was there, because I rarely went a meeting without asking a question or bringing up something controversial. Of course that meant that the administrator running the meeting would hate my presence (for asking a question he /she might not be able or want to answer) as much as all of the other teachers (for asking a question and prolonging the meeting).

Despite trying to get out of attending teachers' meetings, I was forced to attend several hundred in my thirty years as a teacher at Napoleon High School. Many were memorable, including the one that I will describe here.

Larry Long was the Principal at Napoleon High School for six or seven years. Larry is a great person. He cares so much about people that it's easy to get emotional when talking about him. He had a great rapport with the kids. Unfortunately, the faculty at Napoleon High School is darn near impossible to work with. There are/were many, many very intelligent, very outspoken, very stubborn teachers on the staff. It is virtually impossible for an administrator to please the staff at NHS. There are just too many strong-willed people there. Some principals are too tough and the teachers and students hate them. Some principals are too nice to the kids and the teachers hate them.

Some principals are not "academically-oriented" enough and the teachers hate them. It's damn-near impossible to please the entire staff.

Someone once said that if the NHS principal could walk on water one of the teachers would say, "What? He can't swim?"

Okay, so Larry Long is the Principal. A constant problem at Napoleon High School is a lack of security. Napoleon High School is basically the YMCA for the city of Napoleon. Hundreds of people, it seems, have keys to Napoleon High School. Granted, the building is used by the people of Napoleon at all hours of the day and night, so it is inevitable that there will be times when the doors are left unlocked. At least three or four (and usually more) times a year the morning custodian will arrive at NHS and find a door or two left unlocked. These occurrences are always brought up at teachers' meetings.

After years of these occurrences, the school district decided to do something about it. Napoleon High School installed a security system with a touch-pad, alarms, the whole works. Naturally, they had to have a teachers' meeting to explain to the staff how to run the alarm system. It was absolutely crazy. Teachers were going to be able to enter the building near the faculty parking lot. The only security touch-pad at the time was right on the wall inside the door. We were going to have a certain number of seconds to punch in our code to keep the alarm from sounding throughout the building and at the police station which is less than a mile away. Sounds great, huh?

Well, the doors that are often left open, which means outsiders are coming in to use the building, are all the way across the building. Truly, the touch-pad is located as far away from the doors that are used to enter as physically possible in the building. There is absolutely no way in hell for a person to enter the building near the gym and make it to the alarm touch-pad in the time needed. Thus, every time an outsider would come in the building from the gym doors (which are the doors everyone uses and sometimes are left unlocked) the alarm was sure to sound. Wouldn't that be fun? A group of citizens enter the gym for their Sunday night basketball league and the police arrive two minutes later. That would happen every time someone came in the gym. Sounds like a good idea to me, how about you?

So we are at this teachers' meeting and the Principal, Larry Long, goes through the explanation of using the touch-pad, turning off the alarm, etc. He finishes and asks if there are any questions. That is a bad question to ask when I was present at the meeting. My hand shot up and Mr. Long nodded in my direction.

"Let me just say this about that," I started. "Whoever designed this security system had to have his head so far up his butt (I would have said 'ass,' but there were women present) that he couldn't even breathe."

Before the faculty could even nod its collective head in agreement, the Principal said, "That would be me." Oops. I guess I said the wrong thing at the wrong time. The faculty sort of gasped, and then a few of them actually started to laugh and giggle. Hey, that's pretty funny. I felt pretty stupid, and I looked around for a hole to climb into, but Mr. Long was pretty gracious. Let's face it, he probably could have held that against me for years, but it later became a sort of joke between us. At least I think it was considered sort of a joke. I don't really know about Mr. Long. He remains a friend to this day, but on that day things were a little touchy.

Learning At An Early Age

I recently read about a ten-year-old boy who wrote a letter to God. He requested $100 so he could buy his mommy something nice for her birthday. He actually tried to send the letter to 'God.'

The fellows at the local Post Office thought it would be cute to forward the letter to the President, so they did. The President read the letter, thought it was very cute, and put in a five-dollar bill and sent it back to the boy.

The young boy received the gift and wrote back to God. The letter made its way back to the President, who assumed that it was a thank you note. Upon opening the second letter the President read, "Dear God. Thank you for the gift so I can buy my mommy a birthday present. I did notice on the post mark that the letter went through Washington DC. Can you believe it? Those assholes deducted $95 in taxes!"

41

Another Principal Story

The Napoleon High School Principal right before Larry Long was a guy named Don Hummel. He was a no-nonsense, former military man. Players used to say that Vince Lombardi treated all of them alike—like dogs. Well, Don Hummel treated all of his teachers the same—like crap. Actually that's not really true. Don Hummel expected you to do your job. He didn't like whiners and he didn't like people who wouldn't work. He was tough and hard-nosed. All of those traits are good, right? Well, he also didn't have much tact. He called a spade a spade and really didn't care who liked him or didn't like him. Which was good, considering that very few people liked him. I happened to be one of the few who did. I guess I was just brought up to understand that even if you didn't like your boss, he was still your boss.

The other great thing about Don Hummel was his visible support of staff members. If a parent came to school to complain about a teacher, Don Hummel took the side of the teacher in the argument with the parent. He did this 100% of the time. He defended his staff. It's has to be said that he would later call the staff member into his office and oftentimes rip him/her a new asshole, but in front of the public he supported his people.

Now, that being said, he also was a very intimidating fellow. He's about 6-4, and for most of his career wore a gray, flat-top hair-cut. He didn't take any crap from anybody.

All of the coaches at Napoleon High School had the last period of the day scheduled as their conference period. This allowed us to leave school early for athletic contests, prepare for practice, or just unwind at the end of a long school day.

A number of the coaches began playing cards in the teachers' lounge during that final period. One day we were playing Euchre. As I recall, Duane Ressler, Gregg Merrill, Mike King, and I were involved in the game. I know that Don Hummel didn't really like us playing cards, but it was our one free period and he really couldn't do much about it. He just thought that Conference/Planning meant that we were supposed to be working on lesson plans for the next day. Well, we weren't. We were playing Euchre in the teachers' lounge.

The phone system at the time simply had extensions in certain rooms, one of which was the faculty lounge. We were playing cards and the phone rang. Duane Ressler answered the phone. It was Principal Hummel. He was looking for Mike King. Duane paused for a very short second and said, "Mr. King? No, he's not down here."

Duane sat down to continue the game. A few minutes later in walked Don Hummel. I've already told you that he could intimidate the hell out of people. He stepped into the room, looked at our table, pointed to Mike King and used two fingers to signal that he wanted to see him. Mike King got up and went to the office with Don Hummel. The rest of us sat there in stunned silence. A few minutes later we were giggling about it, and, over the years the story has become legendary, but you almost have to see Gregg Merrill motion with those two fingers calling Mike King to the office.

Don Hummel also didn't like a stunt pulled by three science teachers, Mike Hamlin, Jack Schroeder, and Tom Atkinson. The day was a teachers' work-day, which simply meant that the students were gone for the semester or the year, and the teachers were in the building by themselves.

Hamlin, Schroeder, and Atkinson, three of the very best science teachers ever, decided to add a little levity to the boring day. They went out on to the roof of Napoleon High School with water balloons and intended to hit some other faculty members as they returned from lunch. As the teachers approached, it was bombs away. The librarian for the school really didn't appreciate the stunt and complained to the principal. He didn't think it was very funny either.

Later in the day Hamlin and his raiding party went around the school as a SWAT team, this time not only with the water balloons, but also with squirt guns. They hid behind corners of the school attacking some teachers and leaving others alone. When they attacked the same librarian they had previously hit with a water balloon she actually called them "Shitheads." Oooooo. She again complained to the principal.

Principal Don Hummel didn't file a formal complaint against the teachers, but he did something that might have even been worse. We were in the midst of a very tough and serious negotiations for a new contract, and he brought up the incidents at the negotiating table! He wanted us to sign some sort of teachers' discipline code. C'mon!

By the way, despite being really tough and mean, Don Hummel also was pretty darn smart. At the time I was probably the least-liked faculty member (okay, maybe the librarian at the time was liked less than me) because I was basically a student-advocate. I couldn't stand teachers sitting around the faculty lounge complaining about kids. I would frequently remind faculty members that the kids are why we have a job. The students are the most important people in our school, not the teachers. Too many teachers forget that. Hell, we aren't even second. The custodians and the secretaries are way more important than teachers. Schools can't run without custodians and secretaries.

Back to Don Hummel. He trusted me and my opinion on a lot of things. He would call me to his office, close the door, and ask me what I thought of a certain idea. He also knew that I was not very well liked by the other teachers. If I thought his idea was a good one, I would tell him. He would them ask me who I thought we should get to bring the idea up in front of the faculty. I always suggested Mike Hamlin. He was loved by the kids and well-respected by the faculty.

One of Don Hummel's ideas that appeared to come from the faculty (and, eventually ruined by the faculty) was the Student Appreciation Dinner. The faculty prepared spaghetti for an evening dinner in honor of certain students. That was Don Hummel's idea that Mike Hamlin brought up in front of the faculty. Don Hummel was smart enough to know that if he and I brought it up the faculty would immediately hate it, but that if a faculty member came up with the idea the faculty would love it. That's just the way the NHS faculty was, is, and probably always will be. I guess that's not really uncommon.

So, we have this Student Appreciation Dinner. Every teacher was allowed to invite two students. The dinner was free for the students, but the faculty members had to pay $2.00 for every student invited. The first year everybody invited two students, paid, and we all had a great time. Unfortunately, when we went to serve the ice cream for dessert it was almost melted. Earlier in the day somebody had put the ice cream in the refrigerator instead of the freezer.

The next day Mike Hamlin sent out an office memo (this was in the days before e-mail) thanking everyone for their participation and how well everything had gone. He added the line, "Things would have gone much better if some twit hadn't put the ice cream in the refrigerator rather than the freezer."

Later that afternoon, Principal Hummel stopped by Mike Hamlin's room, stepped in, closed the door, and said, "I just want you to know that I was the twit who put the ice cream in the refrigerator instead of the freezer." Hey, at least he didn't do it in front of the entire faculty!

A New Cure For Headaches

A guy was suffering from sever headaches for years with no relief. After trying all of the usual cures he was finally referred to a headache specialist by his family doctor. The specialist asks him for his symptoms and he begins to explain, "I get this sever pain behind my eyes like a knife is slicing into my scalp . . ."

The specialist interrupted the man and said, "And you have a throbbing behind your left ear."

"Yes! Exactly. How did you know?"

"Well, I am the world's greatest headache specialist, and I've seen just about everything as far as headaches go. I myself suffered from that same headache for years. It is caused by a tension in certain muscles on the side of your head. This is how I cured it: Every day I would give my wife oral sex. She would get so excited that she would squeeze her legs together with all her strength and the pressure of her legs would relieve the tension in my head. Try that every day for two weeks and come back and let me know how that works."

Two weeks went by and the man was back. "How do you feel," asked the doctor.

"Doc, I am a new man. I feel great and you are a genius. I haven't had a headache since I started this treatment. I can't thank you enough! And, by the way, you have a lovely home and a nice dog."

42

". . . He's Really Smart."

While I'm at it, I might as well tell you about the maddest I ever saw my very first principal, Mr. Bill Mossing. Bill Mossing, rest his soul, is a legend in Napoleon, Ohio. He started a golf program before most schools would even think about sponsoring golf. He also coached football and basketball and officiated those sports. He was a wonderful man and the principal of Napoleon High School during my first year as a teacher. Bill Mossing had a bald head and when he got upset, which wasn't very often, his head, neck and face would turn a crimson red. I saw that crimson red one day during my first year as a teacher.

I really don't recall what we were talking about in class, but it got around to Adolph Hitler. I asked the class who was responsible for the deaths of the most Jews in history. Naturally, everyone said Hitler. I explained to them that, no, actually Martin Luther was responsible for the deaths of more Jews than even Hitler. It was an innocent comment that I certainly didn't think would cause a stir. However, you need to know that Henry County, Ohio is just about the largest concentration, per capita, of Lutherans in the United States. One of my students went home and told his/her parent that I said that Martin Luther killed twelve million Jews.

The next day I was called down to Mr. Mossing's office. I walked in and he told me to close the door. Remember that I was a first-year teacher. He looked over his desk and said, "Mr. Francis, what this about Martin Luther killing twelve million Jews?"

I tried to explain that it just came up in class and that it was my understanding that Martin Luther was responsible for the deaths of more Jews than Hitler. Mr. Mossing asked me where I got that information.

I'll never forget. My answer was, "My brother-in-law told me. He's really smart."

Mr. Mossing exploded and came right out of his seat. "What!? Your brother-in-law? Don't you realize where you're teaching? You can't go around saying things about Martin Luther. You're in Napoleon, Ohio!"

His face was crimson and I was scared. I tried to interrupt him and he interrupted me instead. "No, no, no. I don't want to hear about it. Just never bring up Martin Luther in class again. Do you hear me?"

I nodded my head and left the office. I immediately went to a phone and called my brother-in-law to get the sources for the information, just in case things went further. I also thought that I would never make it in Napoleon, Ohio. I lasted thirty years teaching and thirty-three coaching. Of course I never brought up Martin Luther in class again, either. At least not in that vein.

The only other time I was called into Mr. Mossing's office (Hey, I only taught under his supervision for one year!) was in late September. I had been hired as the advisor to the school newspaper, *The Wildcats' Roar*. The staff of the student publication had been picked the previous year, and I really didn't know any of the kids very well. They seemed to be good kids, but I also discovered that they were mischievous as well.

The first issue of the newspaper is always published on the day of football homecoming. I was actually pretty proud of the first issue, as the kids and I had worked very hard to get things done correctly. We had to send proofs of the paper to the middle school where they had an offset printing press. The middle school industrial arts teacher actually printed the newspaper and sent it back for the staff to collate and distribute. Once I gave the "OK" to send it to the middle school, the paper was pretty much out of my hands.

Anyway, on the Monday after the first issue, Mr. Mossing sent a note up to my room and asked me to report to his office during my conference period, which happened to be the last period of the day. I went down into his office and knocked on the already-open door.

"Come in Mr. Burke, and close the door," the veteran administrator said.

When the Principal of the school tells you to come in and close the door, you need to immediately get nervous, and I did. I had only been in the building for four or five weeks and here I was being called into the Principal's office.

Mr. Mossing pointed to a seat and said, "Sit down." I did. He handed me a copy of *The Wildcats' Roar* and said, "Can you explain what this means?" On the bottom of page eight there was a single line circled in red. I had no idea, at first, what was circled. When I read what he had circled I almost fainted. There, on the bottom of page eight, it said, "There will be a weenie roast in the boys' restroom after the game tonight."

The blood drained from my head. I gulped. I had no explanation other than to say that once the paper is edited and sent to the middle school I had no control over whether something is added. That could only have been what happened. I could not possibly have missed that on the page before I sent the paper to the printer. I could tell I was stumbling around trying to explain something about smoking in the restroom (which is often a problem at schools), when Mr. Mossing interrupted me and told me to find out how it happened, not to let it happen again, and handle the situation with whomever pulled this little trick.

The next day I really read the riot act to the newspaper staff, most of whom had a tough time not laughing out loud. I tried to explain to them how important trust was and how they just couldn't pull things like this on me. I eventually established a pretty trusting relationship with not only that particular staff, but also newspaper staffs for the next 30 years.

Two For The Senior Citizens

Maude and Claude, both 86 years old, lived in a senior center. They got to talking one day and decided that they liked each other. That night, after bingo, they went back to Claude's room, where, as things sometimes happen, they had a delightful roll in the sack. As they were basking in the glow of the magic moments they had just shared, each was lost for a time in their own thoughts.

Claude was thinking, "I knew she was a spinster and an old maid, but if I had known she was a virgin I would have been more gentle."

Maude was thinking, "If I'd known he could still get it up, I would have taken my panty hose off."

In a large senior citizens home Beatrice loved to get in her wheelchair and race up and down the halls going "Zoom, zoom," with her voice. One day she was doing her "Zoom, zoom," when Delbert stepped out in to the hall. He raised his hand as she was going by. She stopped immediately and he said, "Excuse me, mam, but I noticed you were speeding down the hallway. That's a ticket and is going to cost you ten dollars."

Beatrice reached into a pocket of her robe and took out a receipt she had in her pocket. She smiled and gave it to Delbert. The next time down the hall he stepped out again, put up his hand and said, "Excuse me, mam, but I noticed that you crossed the double yellow line. That will be a ticket and cost you fifteen dollars."

Beatrice smiled and reached into her other pocket and took out another old receipt. The next time she came down the hall Delbert was standing there with his hand up and his robe wide open, revealing a huge erection. Beatrice stopped and said, "Oh no, not the breathalyzer!"

Some Anniversary Stories

An elderly couple got up for breakfast on their 50th anniversary. The wife looked across the table and said, "You know, Honey, we were sitting right here 50 years ago on our wedding day."

The husband smiled a bit and said, "Yeah, but we were probably naked that day."

"So let's get naked right now," the lady said. They both took off all of their clothes.

"You know," she said smiling, "My nipples feel just as hot for you today as they did 50 years ago."

He replied, "They ought to. One's in your tea and the others in your oatmeal."

A couple decided to take their very first cruise to celebrate their 50th anniversary. When they were shown to their stateroom, they walked in and realized that there were bunk beds in the room. They put down their luggage and the husband said, "Up or down?"

The woman tore off all of her clothes and they made mad passionate love. Every evening they would return to their room and he would say, "Up or down," and the woman would attack him, making the best love in their entire marriage.

Upon arriving home from the cruise the old man said, "Honey, I think I'm gonnna buy us some bunk beds."

"Why would you want to do that," she asked.

"Well, on the cruise every time I said, 'Up or down' you attacked me and we made the best love in our entire lives together."

"Oh my god," the lady said. "I thought you were saying 'Fuck or drown.'"

43

Just To Get A Response? Me?

Throughout my teaching career I was often accused of just saying things at teachers' meetings or to other teachers just to get a response from them. I never really thought about doing that. Honest. However, I did ask quite a few questions that were meant to get people thinking. Remember that I have a theory . . . when a teacher goes in to administration he/she has to take numerous very worthwhile classes. Classes with names like "Secondary Administration," "Middle School Administration," "Decision-Making," etc. Oh wait, they don't teach decision-making to administrators, they simply teach them how to write more rules so they can turn to the big black book when something happens to know how to handle it.

My theory is that when a person completes the final class for an administration degree, the college they attend is required to suck out their brains before awarding them the degree. That way, the administrator can say things like, "I can't let you do that. If I let you do that then I have to let everyone do that." Of course those words come out like they are being said by a brainless robot. Yeah, that's it, most administrators sound like brainless robots. But I digress.

Suffice it to say that I was, throughout my teaching career, a student advocate. That means that I took the students' side in most cases dealing with other unreasonable teachers and virtually all administrators. Here are a few examples:

There was an outstanding Social Studies teacher at Napoleon High School who, I am disappointed to tell you, left education (teaching) and went in to administration (no longer education). Before he got his brains sucked out he was, as mentioned, an excellent teacher. He had a real zeal and zest for teaching. He was also loud and obnoxious, but sometimes that actually helps. He was also a former college wrestler and still in great shape—he was coaching the Napoleon wrestling team at the time.

For quite a few years early in my career at Napoleon High School, teachers would gather in the Teachers' Lounge before school to have a cup of coffee, talk, exchange teaching ideas (yeah, right!), etc. One day this excellent teacher was just going on and on about how little motivation his students had. We had actually been trying to do things to motivate kids that year, but he was saying how they weren't working with his students. He went on and on about how 64% of his students had failed his last test. Everybody is listening and sort of nodding theirs heads in the manner of, "Yeah, today's kids just don't work hard enough, blah, blah, blah."

As soon as there was a moment of silence I said, "Boy, Davey, you must be a really shitty teacher."

There was silence in the room for a second or two and then he exploded. "What?!" he yelled.

"Well, hell, obviously you didn't teach them anything. Shit, if 64% of your kids failed that test, then you must not have taught them anything about the information that was on the test." At that point I got kind of scared that he would kick my ass, but I made the point I was trying to make. I even went on to explain it further.

"The way I look at it, if one of my students fails, then I also fail. It's my job to get them to pass, isn't it?" There was again silence in the room. The air was heavy. Davey broke the silence with a roar of laughter.

"I get it, you son of a bitch. You're just trying to play the devil's advocate and get a rise out of me, right?" He roared again with laughter, as did everyone else.

I simply smiled a wry smile and said, "Yeah, Davey, that's what I was doing."

44

The Stephen Francis Rule

Napoleon High School has a school day with eight periods. For the first twenty-five years I taught there just about every teacher taught six periods, had a conference period, and had a duty period. The duty period might be parking lot duty, study hall, or cafeteria supervision, to name a few. One year I had cafeteria supervision. During the first two teacher work days, the Assistant Principal, Delbert Shinn, had numerous meetings. He would have a meeting with the study hall monitors to go over study hall procedures, cafeteria supervisors to go over cafeteria procedures, etc.

Like most people, I hate meetings of any kind, and I especially hate meetings that are a waste of my time when I could be doing something else. So I go to the cafeteria supervisor meeting with a bit of a bad attitude. The Assistant Principal starts to explain that each supervisor (there were four in each lunch period) would be responsible for a specific "quadrant" in the cafeteria. He actually used that word, "quadrant." The meeting was way, way too serious for me.

Once the school year started I would often work through my own lunch period and then head down to my supervision for the other two lunch periods. I would often then go through the cafeteria line when I arrived (teachers get to cut in line—hey, I'm a student advocate, but lunch is lunch!). I would then take a hamburger, hot dog, beef sandwich, etc. to my quadrant where I had to stand and watch kids each lunch.

The next year I also was assigned cafeteria supervision, and, at the pre-school meeting the Assistant Principal said, "We will have a new rule this year during cafeteria supervision," he said. He looked right at me. "If you think this rule is aimed at you, Stephen Francis, you're right. This year there will be no eating in the cafeteria."

Let's just stop there. ". . . there will be no eating in the cafeteria." How stupid is that statement? It reminded me, right then and there, of something my mother had once said at dinner. We were arguing about something and she said to my brother, "Jack Francis, shut your mouth and eat your food." Pretty tough to do, huh?

I naturally wanted to know why he would instigate such a rule, so I asked. "Isn't that a little extreme? In fact, it sounds a little ridiculous if you ask me."

"No one asked you," he snapped. "If you are eating in the cafeteria then you aren't watching your quadrant." There was that word again. I was now ready for a fight.

Immediately after the meeting I went to see the Principal. I went in his office and closed the door. "I need to talk to you about something pretty serious," I said. "I just came from the cafeteria supervisors meeting and Mr. Shinn told us about a new 'Stephen Francis Rule.' No eating in the cafeteria. Did you know about this? What's the deal?"

The Principal, Don Hummel, said, "Yeah, we talked about it. If you use your supervision time for lunch, then other teachers could complain that you are, in fact, getting two lunch periods." That was not the explanation given to me by the Assistant Principal.

"Has anyone actually complained," I asked. "If they do, tell them I'll trade with them and they can have cafeteria supervision and I'll take the extra class."

"No one has complained, and it's more than that. Mr. Shinn thinks that if you're eating you can't be doing your job. Your eyes have to go to your food and away from the kids."

Oh my God! This was getting unbelievable. "So, if I eat without taking my eyes away from the kids, it's okay if I eat?"

He wasn't quite frustrated yet. "I suppose if you eat a cookie or something like that it would be okay."

"A cookie is okay then? How about a hotdog? I think I can eat a hotdog without taking my eyes off of my quadrant," I said with a bit of sarcasm. "How about a bowl of spaghetti? I think I can pick up a spoonful of spaghetti and get it to my mouth without taking my eyes off the kids." I was on a roll. The Principal was just getting to teeth-gritting time.

"Now let's not get ridiculous," he said, temper building.

"No," I snapped, "This already is ridiculous. A cookie is okay. How about an apple? Apple okay? That would make a banana okay, too, right? But not an orange, because I would have to look at it."

"That's enough," he said, raising his voice. "I'll talk to Mr. Shinn."

I'd like to say that things all worked out, but they really didn't. Well, in a way they did, I guess. After that year I never had cafeteria supervision again.

Charm School Graduate

My mother-in-law is a very, very nice person. I was absolutely shocked when she told me this joke, which happens to be very funny and makes a lot of sense.

Four well-to-do rich bitches were sitting around one day talking about their anniversaries. The first lady bragged, "For my twenty-fifth anniversary my husband took me on an eight-week cruise around the world."

The other s oohed and aahed. One lady said, "That's nice. That's very nice."

The next lady said, "Well, for our twenty-fifth anniversary my husband bought me a brand new car. A $63,000 Audi convertible."

Again, they were all impressed and one lady said, "That's nice. That's very nice."

The third lady said, "For our twenty-fifth, my Max bought me this three-carat diamond ring." They were all impressed and the fourth lady again said, "That's nice. That's very nice."

After a few minutes of silence, the other three ladies wanted to know what the fourth lady had received on her anniversary. "For our twenty-fifth, my Harold sent me to Charm School."

"Charm School? Why Charm School?" the other three wanted to know.

The fourth lady answered, "Well, I used to say 'Fuck you, you conniving, stuck-up bitch.' Now I just say, 'That's nice. That's very nice.'"

45

Common Sense Doesn't Always Prevail

In my last few years teaching a new wave of rules entered education in the form of "The Agenda." Students received from the school a small, spiral-bound notebook-type thing with all kinds of pages. The pages included school rules, sports' schedules, bell schedules, calendars for homework assignment, and even some interesting things for kids to read. Students were to carry their agendas at all times as a form of identification.

Near the back of the agendas were pages for teachers to fill out hall passes for students. Teachers were no longer supposed to allow students to roam the hallways without signing their agendas. All that is well and good, and probably a decent security measure for most schools. However, there is one part of the agenda idea that is really funny.

On one of the back pages there are twenty-four lines divided into four sections. The four sections represent the four grading quarters of the school year. The Assistant Principal at the time, Dr. Barbara Ward-Bovee, held up the agenda to explain it to the faculty at another of those delightful pre-school-year teacher meetings. She showed the page with the twenty-four lines and said that those lines were to be filled out by the teachers when the students go to the restroom.

I smiled to myself when she said this. I raised my hand. "So, the students are allowed to use the restroom six times each quarter?" I was working hard to hold back the laughter.

"Yes, that's right," she said.

I lost it, laughing out loud. "Six times a quarter? Hell, I go to the bathroom six times a day!" At that point I noticed that I was the only one laughing. They couldn't be serious, could they? This had to be a well-planned joke just on me. Go to the restroom only six times a quarter? C'mon, that WAS funny, wasn't it?

"We find that there are certain students abusing restroom privileges. There are students who ask to leave study hall every day to use the restroom, and we need to get a handle on this," she explained. I thought that statement was funny in itself. Boys going to the restroom . . . get a handle on it . . . funny stuff. Unfortunately, no one else thought any of this was funny. Her statement that some students were leaving study hall to go to the restroom every day was crazy in itself. Can you think of a better time for students to use the restroom? Did we want them to leave class instead of study hall?

When I stopped laughing I had to ask a follow-up question. I cleared my throat and tried to get serious. "Ok. Six restroom breaks a quarter. If a kid uses all of his restroom breaks before the quarter is over and then had Taco Bell late at night and gets here and really, really has to go . . . we say 'No.' Right?"

Dr. Ward-Bovee was beginning to lose her patience. I wasn't finished.

"I have another question. A serious one. Those passes are supposed to be hall passes, right?" Heads nodded all around. "If I send a kid to the office to pick something up, do I have to use one of the six hall passes for the quarter?" Once again, everyone nodded. "So, if I send a kid to the office to pick up something from you, Dr. Ward-Bovee, he or she now only gets to go to the restroom five times that quarter, right? Isn't that a little extreme? Who will ever want to do a teacher a favor and go to the office?"

Now I had them thinking. Dr. Ward-Bovee looked over at Principal Jeff Schlade. He just looked at her.

"In that case," she said, "I guess you would use one of the blue hall passes."

"Wait. I'm confused. We're still using the blue hall passes?"

"Yes, we can still use the blue hall passes," said the Assistant Principal.

"Then why do we have the agendas," I asked. "Why not just fill out the blue hall passes for the restroom?" They explained that the agendas were to serve as identification for the students so that we know where everyone is at all times.

I was still on a roll. "Why not eliminate the blue hall passes? On the back side of the restroom page is another page of hall passes. Why not save a tree or two and just use the back for hall passes and the front for restroom passes?" You will not believe the response.

"Oh, that's way too confusing. We'll never be able to keep straight if someone is using more than their share of passes."

I actually stood up and took one of the agendas. I held it up in front of everybody and showed them the one page with two sides for passes. "Let me see if I can get this. This side for hall passes." I turned the page. "This side for restroom passes. Hall passes. Restroom passes. Hall passes. Restroom passes. I think I got it."

At that point everybody was mad at me for taking time during a meeting to bring up something so, so, so ridiculous. Wait a minute. I didn't bring it up, I just responded to what was already ridiculous.

Section V

The Funniest Thing . . . .

46

"Don't Make No Difference . . . ."

Here it is, the funniest thing I ever heard . . . .

I have a friend who retired from teaching quite a few years ago. He had traveled all over the country and had seen just about all there was to see. In his last few years teaching he had continually told all of his fellow teachers that all he wanted to do when he retired was to own a log cabin in the mountains somewhere.

When he retired he started looking to buy some land somewhere in the mountains. The best price he could find was for sixteen acres in the mountains deep in West Virginia. He was so excited. He bought a small camper and lived in the camper on his land for the six months it took him to build his house. The place turned out to be just about everything he ever wanted.

He had lived in the finished home for a few months and hadn't really talked to anyone in the area, as the cabin was in a pretty remote area. One afternoon during the summer he was sitting on his long front porch reading, drinking a beer, and smoking his pipe. He noticed an old, beat-up pick-up truck pulling up his long, unpaved driveway. There was dust flying all over the place as the truck pulled right up near his house.

A guy got out of the truck, adjusted his coveralls (only one strap was attached), and walked toward my friend. The stranger had on old boots with no laces and no socks. His hair was dirty and greasy, and when he began to talk my friend noticed he only had a few teeth.

The stranger stepped up on to the porch and spoke first. "Ya'll must be my new neighbor."

My friend nodded and said, "Yeah, I guess so. I've been here for a few months."

"I wanna invite you to a party."

"Cool," my friend nodded. "I like parties. What's going on?"

"Well," the guy continued. "Gonna be some drinkin.' Gonna be some dancin.' Gonna be some fightin.' Gonna be some fuckin.'"

"Wow," said my friend. "That sounds like lots of fun. Count me in. Say, what does someone wear to a party like that?"

The hillbilly just shook his head. "Don't make no difference. Just gonna be you and me."

47

He Was Actually Ducking

The funniest thing I ever saw occurred in the Arcade of The Excalibur Hotel and Casino in Las Vegas. My brothers and sisters joined my mother for her birthday in Las Vegas in 1995. My brothers Jack and Bob aren't too much into gambling, but they really like to have a good time, and Las Vegas is a place where you can have a great time without gambling.

On morning we were touring different resorts and we ended up in the Arcade at The Excalibur. It was a great time. We played all sorts of driving games, games of skill and chance, and we then found an Old West saloon game where the player had a gun and had to shoot and kill the bad guys as they came out of the saloon.

My brother Bob, who fancies himself quite a shot with a pistol, was playing this game. It's important to understand that this is a video game, and the bad guys are just on the screen. He was shooting at the bad guys and they were shooting back. They weren't of course, actually shooting back, but he was dodging and ducking as if the shots were coming through the screen.

I realize that we had had a bit to drink, and that this was clearly a "had-to-be-there" moment, but watching my brother try to not get shot while playing a video game was the funniest thing ever. He wasn't messing around, either, he was being serious in trying to dodge the bullets as they weren't being shot back. The scene was so funny that I fell to the floor of the arcade. I thought I was having a heart-attack I was laughing so hard.